THE WHITE HOUSE
in PICTURE and STORY

BY JOSEPH LEEMING

NEW YORK, N. Y.

GEORGE W. STEWART · PUBLISHER · INC.

TO THE WHITE HOUSE

"There is probably no building in the world where more history has centered than in this shining White Mansion. Heroic men have died here. . . . There have been marriages and merry makings, too, jovial feasts and ceremonial banquets; grave councils of state that shaped the destiny of the nation, secret intrigue, midnight conclaves that made or unmade political parties, war councils that flashed forth orders which moved great armies and set lines of battle in deadly front. The history of the White House is a . . . history of the United States from 1800 to this day."

E. V. Smalley, 1884

Second Edition, March 1954

COPYRIGHT, 1953, BY
GEORGE W. STEWART, PUBLISHER, Inc.

Library of Congress Catalog Card Number: 53-6172

ACKNOWLEDGMENTS

To follow the far reaching and complex history of the White House, for even so brief a story as the present volume, would have been impossible without the help of those who have been associated with the house, foundations that have been established to preserve some of its memorabilia and some of our great libraries where books, letters, prints and photographs are maintained by informed and gracious custodians. Many individuals have taken time and trouble to help fill an incomplete record.

For his gracious and copious help I am especially indebted to Laurence Gouverneur Hoes, great grandson of President Monroe, for photographs and information about the Monroe furniture and household accessories, many of which are preserved in the James Monroe Memorial Foundation, Fredericksburg, Va. To Ruth Woodworth, Curator of the President Benjamin Harrison Home, I am indebted for the use of their pictures of Harrison's White House rooms. Dare Stark McMullin gave me the use of her photograph of the Hoover's Second Floor Oval Room and colorful, helpful details of Mrs. Hoover's contribution to the White House furnishings. Grace Coolidge kindly solved the mystery of the Red and Green Room seal rugs.

I am grateful to the National Capital Parks and to the Library of Congress, Prints and Photographs Division, for their help in obtaining photographs, and to Margareth Jorgesen of the National Archives for her patient and ready assistance in verifying many details. Thomas Little, of the Theodore Roosevelt Collection, Harvard College Library, lent many photographs that helped identify period details of decoration. The staff of the Art Reference Room and History Room of the New York Public Library were most cooperative in my research.

To Charles T. Haight, director of the B. Altman & Company decorating department, and his associate, Peggy Watts, I am indebted for their most generous gift of time and their painstaking answers to my many detailed questions about the 1952 decorating, also to Douglas Hahn for his permission to reproduce B. Altman decorating sketches. R. Curt Hasenclever, of F. Schumacher & Co., enthusiastically shared his time and information about decorative fabrics and supplied photographs of some. Richard Dillon, of Scalamandré, and Frank Judson, Jr., of Stroheim & Romann, kindly supplied the pictures and histories of other fabrics. Robert J. Sullivan, of Lenox China, supplied photographs of some of the Presidential china shown. Marie Kimball's imaginative reconstruction of the furnishings of the early rooms was most helpful. Ruth Davidson, of *Antiques Magazine*, Elinor Hillyer, of *Woman's Home Companion*, and Eleanor Johnston, of *House and Garden*, graciously gave me information. Bess Furman answered many questions. Herbert Hoover's secretarial staff helped locate information.

Many other persons have helped with a fact here, an anecdote there. Books, magazine files and newspapers old and new have contributed legend and records. In the interest of brevity I could only digest a great body of fascinating material and try to present characteristic or representative items.

I wish also to acknowledge the continued work and cooperation of Eleanor Warren Stewart whose professional training in interior design has made possible this study of the past and present furniture and decorations in the story of the White House.

J. L.

Washington, D. C.
November 1952

ONE NIGHT in January, 1948, President Harry S. Truman, with his wife Bess, was receiving in the Blue Room of the White House. As he shook the hand of each guest and spoke to him, Mr. Truman became aware of a strange sound. Through the pleasant hubbub of the party he clearly heard an ominous tinkling of the chandelier which, like Damocles' sword, hung directly over his and Mrs. Truman's heads.

Harry Truman did not miss a handshake but his eyes sought out Mr. W. E. Reynolds, Commissioner of Public Buildings. As soon as the last person had been welcomed he hurried to the Commissioner. That night they found ample evidence to prove that the venerable White House was in an alarmingly unsafe condition.

The White House architect, Lorenzo Winslow, was called in. Thorough investigations with shocking discoveries followed. The brick supports to the stairway where hundreds of people daily tramped up and down were crumbling. The East Room ceiling was sagging about six inches due to rotting timbers. Temporary support had to be given it at once. A brick column needed to hold up the roof support was falling apart, and the roof itself could easily have collapsed without warning. The floors and ceilings of most of the rooms were sagging and shaky.

While investigations were going on, one leg of Margaret Truman's piano went through the floor of her sitting room, breaking through the ceiling below.

The brick inner walls, with no other base than the clay soil the house stood on, had sunk, cracking plaster and bending floors as they settled. Entire walls leaned toward the center of the building. Massive floor beams were dangerously honeycombed with borings for pipes and conduits and wires required for water, gas, heating and electricity and telephone and signaling systems. The sandstone outer walls, with foundations only five feet deep and resting on clay, had sunk and shifted. Even a slight earth tremor could have turned the whole building into a tragic heap of rubble.

There were two years of discussion and indecision. Was the building worth saving? Should they scrap the whole thing and build a new White House? What about a new site? Finally the Commission decided (and a great many citizens all over the country were relieved by the decision) to rebuild and restore the old White House.

During part of this time Mr. and Mrs. Truman and Margaret were on a nation-wide campaign tour. When they came back to Washington it was to Blair House across Pennsylvania Avenue. The White House had been judged too unsafe to be lived in.

In March 1952, the Trumans were able to return, just in time to receive Queen Juliana and Prince Bernhard of the Netherlands as their first house guests in the newly reconditioned White House.

Photo Courtesy National Park Service

Aerial view, 1937, showing how L'Enfant's plan developed with radiating avenues.

George Washington
1789-1797

Executive Mansion in New York, 1785-1790, Philadelphia, 1790-1800, Washington, D.C., 1800.

In 1902 stones were uncovered in the original construction bearing workmen's initials and Masonic emblems. In 1952 they were used in rebuilding fireplaces in the Communications Room.

L'Enfant's plan radiating streets from monuments and important buildings has proved a

More than 150 years earlier, October 1792, the cornerstone was laid for the White House, the first permanent residence of the Presidents. The Masons conducted the ceremony with George Washington officiating. From the beginning of the new nation the location of the capital city had been an honor contended for by North and South and each state. The problem finally was settled by forming the District of Columbia. Located there the city was a part of no state, midway between the North and the South and central to all the states then existing. George Washington is said to have chosen the site for the city and the location of the President's Palace.

Physically the choice was not an altogether happy one. Although nearby Georgetown and Alexandria were well established, Washington was an unimproved "wilderness" of forest and swamp lands. Its polluted streams and poor drainage endangered health for many years. The climate with its humid summers and unseasonal blizzards (they have an uncanny way of coming at Inauguration time) still complicates the city's work and social life. But its natural beauties—its trees and its fine river views—are compensations. Pierre L'Enfant made a brilliant and orderly plan for the city. Sanitation

6

Hoban's prize winning drawing for the President's House, 1792.

improved over the years and today, in spite of its climate, Washington is the pride of the land.

The Founding Fathers, men of taste and breeding and high patriotism, wanted the residence of their First Citizen to have no hint of regal splendor. But they felt that America's center of diplomatic and state social life must have importance and inspiring beauty. James Hoban's design combined these qualities with simplicity. It won for him the $500.00 prize for the best design for a President's House and the job of superintending its building.

The Duke of Leinster's Palace, in Dublin, has often been thought to be Hoban's inspiration for the White House; but it seems more likely that he based his design on one for a "Gentleman's House," which it closely resembles, in a book of architecture by James Gibbs. Architectural books were being brought here from England in large numbers and were widely used. By mastering and adapting the beautiful Georgian designs and details, architects and craftsmen raised American architecture of that day to a high level.

George Washington said, "I found at Georgetown many well conceived and ingenious plans for the Public buildings in the New City; it was a pleasure indeed, to find, in an infant Country, such a display of architectural abilities."

The Commission wanted to cut the size of both the house and grounds, believing a smaller President's House better suited to the democratic principles of the nation and to its budget.

Would it be economy to base the plans for the President's Palace on the needs of the infant nation? Washington thought not.

> . . . "For the President's House, I would design a building which should also look forward, but execute no more of it at present than might suit the circumstances of this Country when it shall be first wanted. A plan comprehending more may be executed at a future period when the wealth, population, and importance of it shall stand upon much higher ground than they do at present."

serious problem to modern traffic.

Everyone agreed on Washington as the name of the city. It became official after George Washington's death.

Beginning of two political parties: Federalists headed by Hamilton and Republicans by Jefferson. Washington acted as referee between parties. Both urged him to take Presidency for second term.

Washington favored internal revenue tax and national bank to reduce 54 million dollar war debt.

Declared U.S. neutral in war of 1793 between France and England to avoid involving the new nation. This declaration became national policy for over 100 years.

Jefferson anonymously entered in the contest his own classic design for a President's House. Unnoticed by the judges, years later it was found by his grandson among Jefferson's papers.

Building was started at once but due to difficulties in obtaining materials and money it took 8 years.

The White House was the first building started in Washington, the Capitol a year later.

James Hoban designed a fine Georgian mansion, a central building balanced by flanking wings, with gracefully proportioned and spacious rooms. The simple restrained elegance which Hoban created has given lasting dignity and beauty to the White House. As it stands today its form and plan and dimensions are his.

The test of the forefathers' planning came in 1948 when there was talk of razing the old White House and building a new one. The people protested. The old White House represented some of the finest architecture of its period. After one hundred and fifty years it remained, a monument to the citizens' faith and pride in the new nation. Enriched by its associations it had become a national symbol dear to the American people.

Swayed by public opinion the Commission decided to retain the old walls intact and to return the interior to its established plan. They would keep the best of the changes made by the long succession of Presidents who had lived there. They would take this oppor-

Looking east along south wall during excavation.

Photo by Abbie Rowe—Courtesy National Park Service

Three giant bulldozers worked inside the 22 foot deep excavation; the walls became an empty shell. Steel beams were hauled through doors and windows for a whole new framework.

Electric ducts and outlets, air-conditioning, pipes and conduits, had to be placed to a most exacting plan to be in precise locations when the details of the old rooms were restored.

To restore the building was a gigantic undertaking. Everything useful was labeled, packed, stored: mahogany doors, door trim, knobs, locks, windows, window frames, all marble on the first floor; the elevator and kitchen equipment.

Quantities of unusable materials, bricks, woodwork, stone, metal, old nails, were sold at handling cost to thousands of people as souvenirs.

Molds of the ornamental plasterwork in the State Rooms made faithful reproductions possible.

tunity to make the White House thoroughly modern structurally and mechanically.

The sagging floors were removed. The weakened inside brick walls and partitions were torn away. Bricks and mortar came down under the impact of pneumatic drills and sledge hammers. The house completely gutted, bulldozers dug out the earth beneath the old ground floor. Twenty-two feet down they went to make room for two basements, one above the other.

A solid foundation must go below the soft surface clay to the hard sand and gravel level. About 24 feet below the surface one hundred and twenty huge concrete piers were put in place. On these piers a strong steel framework was built to support the floors and roof, anchored at intervals to the original outer stone walls by tie rods to bind the entire structure together. A whole new house was erected in this frame within the old walls.

To visitors who do not know the extent of the 1952 rebuilding, the White House seems practically the same as it was. The exterior shows little or nothing of what has gone on. Excavations were leveled over, workmen's temporary shacks removed, the lawns resodded. Rooms were returned to their original dimensions, with their trim and woodwork nearly, if not identical. To the casual eye rooms in which the furniture and decorations remained the same seem undisturbed. Where changes were made, early Federal styles were used.

When the White House was first built in 1800 only the central building was erected, without the now familiar porticos and wings. Hoban's design called for these additions later and for economy there were two floors above the ground floor instead of the planned three. Even in this simpler form some patriots felt that the new President's Palace was over fine. They feared it might set the President apart.

Moreover they objected to saying "the President's Palace" and by 1800 the White House was generally called the President's House or, because of its elegance, the President's Mansion. From 1818 to 1902 the home of the President was officially known as the Executive Mansion but more and more it was commonly called the White House. In 1902 Congress made that name official and President Theodore Roosevelt had *The White House* engraved on the official stationery and used it in all official communications.

George Washington is the only President who did not live in the White House. His term expired March 4, 1797. But his interest in the White House continued and he made his last inspection of it a few months before his death in December 1799.

The following November the White House was considered ready for occupancy. John Adams and his wife, Abigail, were its first tenants. Mrs. Adams's letter to her daughter dated November 21,

Not only were English styles an inherited taste of the early citizens, but books by foremost furniture makers like Chippendale, Adams and Sheraton inspired American makers —Savery, Phyfe and others. The Commission chose in these styles for the 1952 restoration.

Possibly the name *White House* came from the white paint used to cover the smoke-blackened walls after the burning in 1814. But in a letter King George III ordered General Ross to sack the city and burn the important buildings, naming the White House. And other early letters suggest that George Washington so named it in honor of Martha for her own house in Virginia where he courted her.

John Adams
1797-1801

9

Had been Vice President 8 years

A Federalist, he was opposed throughout his term by both his Vice President Jefferson and Federalist leader Hamilton.

Served more than 3½ years of his term in the President's House in Philadelphia.

War with France barely avoided by treaty.

Enlarged Navy: increased taxes.

Alien and Sedition Acts 1798. Years later seceding Southern States disastrously applied its principle of the right of states to act independently of the Federal government.

Abigail Adams managed both her own and her husband's extensive properties in Massachusetts.

Drawing room was the term in common use for the smaller receptions, a *levee* was a large reception, often open house.

Adams and Jefferson died on the same day,

1800 (it is said to be the first letter written in the White House) gives us the clearest picture of the President's House as they found it.

"... the river, which runs up to Alexandria, is in full view of my window, and I see the vessels as they pass and repass. The house is upon a grand and superb scale, requiring about thirty servants to attend and keep the apartments in proper order. The work of lighting the apartments, from the kitchen to parlors and chambers, is a tax indeed; and the fires we are obliged to keep to secure us from daily agues are another very cheering comfort. ... bells are wholly wanting, not one single bell being hung through the whole house, and promises are all you can obtain. ... If they will put me up some bells, and let me have wood enough to keep fires, I design to be pleased. ... there is not a single apartment finished. ... We have not the least fence, yard, or other convenience, without, and the great unfinished audience-room I make a drying-room of, to hang up the clothes in. The principal stairs are not up, and will not be this winter. Six chambers are made comfortable. ..."

But she finishes: "It is a beautiful spot, capable of every improvement and the more I view it the more I am delighted with it."

Some of the things the Adamses were bringing with them from Philadelphia were stolen and much of their china was broken in the move. There were not enough furnishings left to fill even the six finished rooms, and little money seems to have been allowed for more. But January 1, 1801, John and Abigail Adams held a housewarming. The sparsely furnished rooms were brightened with lighted lamps and candles and warmed with blazing fires for which they had somehow managed to get wood. This was the first full scale reception in the White House. They received in the attractive upstairs Oval Room (now the President's Study) where they had put the crimson covered mahogany chairs and sofas and had hung the crimson damask draperies they had brought with them.

Mrs. Adams was an exceptional woman, socially experienced in America and Europe. She had an intelligent and lively interest in all the affairs of State. Her championship of votes for women and the abolition of slavery were advanced opinions for the times.

In their short three months Abigail Adams had the White House running smoothly. She established a formal social order with her weekly drawing rooms, continuing here in the "Wilderness city" the courtly etiquette of the President's houses in New York and Philadelphia. It was a stiff and ceremonious style of entertaining. Both Abigail Adams and Martha Washington received seated. The President did not shake hands with his guests but bowed from the waist. Their dress was elegant and elaborate.

These early Presidents wanted to be democratic but the influence of European patterns was still strong. And John Adams, who had lived in London as our Minister, agreed with much of the British conduct of both political and social affairs.

Many of the other leaders were quite as confused. They sincerely wanted each man to be a plain citizen, the equal of every other man. But they had grown up accustomed to courtly deference and rituals

An 1807 drawing, the only picture of the White House before the British burned it.

in high offices. How much form and ceremony must there be in the **President's House** to show other nations and their own countrymen the importance of the new Republic? How much form could they discard in the interest of the new equality of man?

For Thomas Jefferson there was no such conflict. He was deeply devoted to the new Republic and was fearless in promoting whatever he felt would advance the principles of democracy. He was widely

July 4, 1826, just fifty years after both signed the Declaration of Independence.

Thomas Jefferson 1801-1809

Author of the Dec-

1809 plan for the first floor, drawn by Latrobe after Hoban.

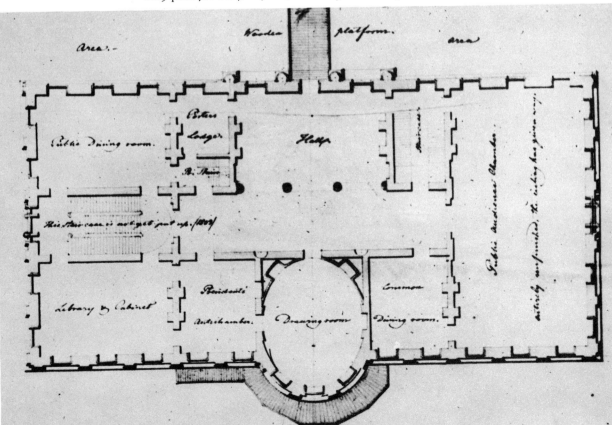

Sketch for the North and South Porticoes as designed by Jefferson and Latrobe, 1807.

laration of Independence.

Tied Aaron Burr in bitterly contested election. Congress elected Jefferson as "less dangerous."

Jefferson had been our minister to France for several years.

Our most famous amateur architect, he designed in this style his own home, Monticello, the original group of buildings for the University of Virginia, and six or more houses for his friends. The idea caught on rapidly and spread over the country, developing a truly American architectural style based on the Classic.

The elite of Washington deprived of their exclusive right to the entertainment of the White House felt injured. But when a group of socially privileged ladies called to assert their rights Mr. Jefferson welcomed them

popular, realistic and practical, and bristled with ideas.

The phenomenal spread of Classic architecture in America at this time was largely due to Jefferson's influence. He saw his own country in the ideas and traditions of the Roman Republic. He believed that young America should do what the young French Republic had done and discard the elaborate styles of the Renaissance and adopt the simpler Classic styles as a symbol of Republican democracy. He encouraged architects who favored classicism.

Jefferson left his lasting mark on the architecture of the White House. When the house was being built he had worked closely with Washington and Hoban. Now with the help of Benjamin Latrobe, architect and engineer, whom he had brought to Washington as Surveyor of Public Buildings, Jefferson redesigned the South Portico to give it its broad sweeping steps. Together they also revised the design for the North Portico, giving it the beautiful rising columns we know today.

Where Hoban's plan called for wings on the east and west Jefferson built terraces and colonnades similar to the servants' wings in Monticello. These were to provide protected promenades with rooms within for storage of fuel and provisions, overlooked in the original plan. To the west, in the same location as today's executive wing, Jefferson had a small office built for himself.

Thomas Jefferson, though born and brought up an aristocrat, believed that society must be levelled. At once he did away with the formal "Drawing Rooms" and his doors were never closed to anyone at "any reasonable hour." He planned for only two great reception days a year, one on New Year's Day and one on Independence Day. To these everyone was welcome.

President Jefferson received all visitors easily and casually. He was known to keep diplomats waiting while he chatted with American Indians who had come to see the Great White Father; and when he finally received his distinguished guests he might appear in worn-out house slippers and carefully careless attire.

Jefferson was bent upon not allowing one's personal station to appear higher than another's. In this cause he angered the British Ambassador Merry and his wife by offering his arm to Mrs. Madison, his hostess, instead of to the ranking Mrs. Merry. To the Ambassador this amounted to an insult to his country. Jefferson seemed to be unaware of the international uproar that followed. Scathing and ridiculing letters were written. The James Monroes (Monroe was then our Minister to England) were snubbed by the British to even the score. There was gossip on both sides of the ocean. Jefferson accepted this slanderous talk willingly so long as it fed his reputation for simplicity. By his insistence on equality Jefferson strengthened democratic thinking and customs throughout the nation for all time.

In the White House, Jefferson surrounded himself with the furnishings and manner of living he had always known, in spite of his belief in "republican simplicity." He abandoned his careless attire and dressed handsomely when he wished. He brought from Monticello a staff of servants and many treasured art objects. He even brought a coachman and "four blooded bays," although it is said that he seldom used them except when his daughters were visiting him.

His many-sided interests spread to every detail of the furnishings of the White House. Because he kept careful records we know that he furnished completely twenty-three rooms. But the pieces were described simply as "elegant" or "gilt" or "mahogany" and the style of most of it can only be guessed at. Since Jefferson was always in the vanguard of fashion it is reasonable to assume that he had furniture made in the popular styles of the day: the English Adams, Sheraton and Hepplewhite or the French Louis XVth and XVIth and Directoire. Probably much of it was painted or gilded or both.

In the forthright qualities of cotton fabrics Jefferson found another expression of simplicity. He had learned to know and like the copper-plate prints on cotton so popular in Europe and had brought *toile de Jouy* to Monticello. In the White House he introduced the use of cottons for draperies in State rooms to replace the usual silks.

For the important floors he used hand loomed Brussels carpets. But many of the floors including the large entrance hall were covered with painted canvas.

The rooms Jefferson planned were a curious mixture of elegance and simple homeliness, with a dash of the unexpected. His Cabinet room, which he made to his personal taste, held a long center table with drawers on each side where he kept official papers and documents and where he also kept a set of carpenter's tools and a small set of garden tools which it amused him to use.

"Around the walls were maps, globes, charts, books, etc. In the window

warmly, as he did everyone, his charm making them quite forget their demands.

He "often flashed out . . . in his white coat, breeches and vest and white silk hose fit to figure on a Watteau fan."

His inventories show five pairs of chintz for the President's drawing room and two pairs of chintz for the small dining room.

Painted canvas was a popular floor covering in the early part of the century, used in the minor rooms in the White House for many years.

Muslin and linen, green baize, straw matting and oilcloth were inventoried as floor coverings through most of the 19th Century.

His enjoyment of designing and his love of convenience were responsible for his many ingenious devices, among them his clothes machine and the revolving circular shelves (a forerunner of the "Lazy Susan" shelves we use in kitchens today).

13

U.S. fleet sent to Tripoli ended their recurring interference with American trading ships.

Louisiana Territory purchased from France for 15 million dollars.

Lewis & Clark Expedition sent to report on riches of this territory.

Land rights taken from Indians east of Mississippi River, forcing them West.

Embargo act passed. In practice hurt U.S. industries more than British trade.

Planted the White House grounds with native trees.

James Madison
1809-1817

Called the "father of the Contitution" because he drafted most of it. Chief advocate of the "Bill of Rights."

Mrs. Madison's sewing table.

recesses were stands for the flowers and plants which it was his delight to attend and among his roses and geraniums was suspended the cage of his favorite mocking-bird, which he cherished with peculiar fondness, not only for its melodious powers, but for its uncommon intelligence and affectionate disposition."

The great East Reception Room was still unfinished. But at last the first floor Oval Reception Room (known now as the Blue Room) was ready. Jefferson held here his first big reception on the Fourth of July 1801. At this time he started the democratic custom of hand-shaking which has continued, often a painful ordeal to the President who has thousands of hands to shake but a valued symbol to the citizen of a man-to-man meeting.

President Jefferson's two married daughters, either of whom could have graced the White House, were occupied with bringing up their young families—a job their father felt to be far more important than being White House hostess. Jefferson on occasion asked the wives of his Cabinet members to assist him. But it was the vivacious and capable Dolley Madison, wife of James Madison, his Secretary of State, who usually served as his hostess. The combination of her wit and easy good nature and his personal charm and popularity made the Jefferson administration a "continual levee." There were always guests at his table for whom he provided lavishly, so lavishly that at the end of his administration he was in debt and it was only through the consideration of his friends that he was able to live again at his beautiful Monticello.

When James Madison became President, Dolley Madison was an experienced First Lady. She shortly became one of the most famous hostesses Washington has ever known. It has always been the privilege of the incoming President and his wife to freshen and rearrange the White House to their taste within the available budget and the restrictions of tradition. Dolley Madison lost little time. For the Oval Reception Room, with the help of Benjamin Latrobe, she selected new sofas and high backed chairs and had them upholstered in sunflower yellow satin with damask window draperies to match. They bought a guitar and mirrors to make a lively background for the weekly Drawing Rooms which Mrs. Madison re-established. There were levees again, once a week, and they held the usual big receptions, as well, on New Years' and Independence Days.

James Madison, a man of slight stature, was highly intelligent and independent, but he lacked the gift of attracting people which is so important in the diplomatic life of the President. This Dolley supplied with her affability and good looks. Madison was content to let her take the limelight. At their weekly dinners she presided at the head of the table, the service elegant with the new china and silver and a servant stationed behind each guest. Madison as a rule sat halfway down the side where he missed nothing, enjoying his wife's easy, skillful social grace. But in small groups, friends found the intelligent James Madison witty and endearing.

On August 24, 1814, a British force captured the city of Washington and burned the President's House, the Capitol and other public buildings. President Madison had, the day before, gone to meet General Winder, expecting to return the following day. As the British drew nearer, Dolley was urged to leave for her safety. But she waited for her husband until she had been repeatedly implored to go. If the spirited Dolley had had her way they would never have abandoned the White House but would have defended it "with a cannon from every window."

The story is often told that Dolley cut the famous Lansdowne Stuart painting of George Washington from its frame, rolled it under her arm and fled with it to the Virginia woods. Actually, the rescued painting of Washington is not the one commissioned by Lord Lansdowne but another by Gilbert Stuart. Nor does the canvas show evidence of having been cut from its frame. Mrs. Madison, packed and ready to leave the White House, wrote in a letter that to avoid delay in unscrewing the painting from the wall she had "ordered the frame broken and the canvas taken out" and the picture given to "two gentlemen from New York" for safe-keeping. They were true to their trust, since this painting now hangs in the White House for all to see.

When the Madisons came back to Washington three days later they found only "part of the walls and the vaulting that supports some of the floors" of the President's House remaining. For the balance of his term Madison set up an Executive Mansion in the nearby Octagon House. Here, with makeshift furniture and Dolley's ingenuity, the diplomatic life continued smoothly and with sparkle but without luxury.

Courtesy Smithsonian Institution

Hepplewhite chair used by President Madison in the White House.

The Lansdowne was secured for the Pennsylvania Academy of the Fine Arts, Philadelphia, in 1811.

For her lifetime Mrs. Madison was social head of the capital, honored by visiting diplomats.

"To be popular with a man you must feed and flatter him," was a Dolley Madison maxim. Dolley did both.

She affected turban-type headdress, often French, feathered and jeweled.

War of 1812. Outraged by England's high-handed sea policies, America declared war.

Brilliant naval victories won peace, 1814, and European governments' esteem.

Encouraged manufacturers, protective tariff, national system of roads and canals.

Little but the walls of the White House were left standing after the burning by the British, shown in this 1816 sketch of St. John's Episcopal Church.

This Louis XVI writing table, mahogany with metal inlay and mounts, is part of Monroe's furniture which he took to the White House. His portrait is by Rembrandt Peale. The silhouettes are of President and Mrs. Monroe, and the box and candelabrum were theirs.

James Monroe
1817-1825

Six new states added to the Union.

Florida purchased.

Monroe Doctrine warned foreign powers against interference with South and Central American republics.

The Missouri Compromise, permitting slaves in Missouri but no other Louisiana Purchase Territory, postponed North and South conflict.

In 1815, again under the direction of James Hoban, the rebuilding of the White House to its original plan was begun. It was not finished until after James Monroe had succeeded to the Presidency. During the restoration the blackened walls were given the coating of thick white paint which, if it did not originate the name of the White House, at least added new meaning to it. And with the reconditioning of the building, Hoban built for the first time the graceful South Portico, using his plan as it was modified by Jefferson and Latrobe.

In the fall of 1817 the work of rebuilding the White House so progressed that James Monroe and his family were able to move in. The only government owned furnishings were the totally inadequate pieces the Madisons had used in the Octagon House. It was necessary therefore to start all over again on the complicated task of furnishing the White House. Because of his background of wealth and diplomatic service abroad, James Monroe was convinced that if a more elegant and formal diplomatic social routine were followed, the foreign nations would be quicker to accept and esteem the

The Astor piano, the mirror, the chairs, and the candlestand were used by the Monroes in the White House.

upstart Republic. He set about to make of the White House a suitable background, as he saw it. To avoid delays the Monroes had brought much fine furniture, silver, china, glassware and decorations from their own home. This the government appraised and bought from Monroe at their own figure. For months before workmen were busy refinishing, reupholstering and repairing it. There was enough of this furniture to furnish the less important drawing rooms and the more important bedrooms, and their beautiful mahogany chairs and tables were well suited to State dining. To insure proper service they brought also their staff of liveried Negro servants.

Mrs. Monroe's bed was a square fourposter with hangings of green, fringe-trimmed cambric, the same green cambric being used with undercurtains at the windows. It was customary in fine houses to use muslin undercurtains, often heavily fringed. The Monroes used them in every room of the White House.

From France the Monroes ordered elegant chairs, sofas and tables and many fine decorations and fittings. They ordered clocks, vases, mirrors, sconces and chandeliers, and richly beautiful fabrics for draperies and upholstery.

The Blue Room

James and Elizabeth Monroe, like Jefferson and the Madisons before them, furnished the first floor Oval Reception Room (the Blue Room) for their most important entertaining. They chose a color scheme of red and gold, using light crimson for upholstery

South Portico was not completed until 1824.

Monroe had been Minister to both France and England.

The Monroes furnished the legation in Paris in beautiful French Empire furniture. Brought it to their Washington house when Monroe was at the same time both Secretary of State and War under Madison. Their house escaped the burning and it was this furniture, in perfect harmony with the architecture of the White House, which they took there in 1817.

Monroe bought busts of Washington, Columbus, Amerigo Vespucci, formerly in Mount Vernon.

17

Nothing less than gold seemed proper to their agent in France, who wrote "mahogany is not generally admitted in the furniture of a saloon even at a private gentleman's house."

Some of their "extravagances" have been in continuous use and are prized possessions of the White House.

A rug of closely similar design and coloring preserved in Mount Vernon was used by Washington in the President's Palace in Philadelphia. This may have inspired the design which Monroe sent to the makers of the Oval Room rug.

In 1857 Buchanan replaced Monroe's gilt furniture in the Blue Room with gilt furniture of domestic make in the French manner. Its lines and proportions show lessening of fine design.

No one seems to know what became of Monroe's gilt furniture.

and draperies. In color it was similar to the Adams's furnishings. But there the similarity ceased.

The Monroe's handsome importations were in the style of the French First Empire. The wood of the chairs and sofas was carved with branched olive leaves and gilded. The sofas were nine feet long with curved ends and two matching separate down cushions for each. There were two large gilt armchairs with down backs and seats and eighteen smaller ones, as well as stools and tabourettes. The laurel leaf motif on the delicately colored crimson satin used for the upholstery was in two tones of gold accenting the gold of the frames.

Crisp taffeta in matching light crimson was draped fashionably from the eagle-topped gilded cornices at the windows. The room was lighted with a gilt bronze chandelier, four arms in the form of an eagle, hung with glittering crystals holding fifty candles. There were candelabra and branching sconces. The clock used on the mantel shows Minerva leaning on a shield, the base heavily decorated with military trophies. At each side of the clock were vases decorated with engraved landscapes. The hearth fittings and andirons were of gilt and handsomely ornate. There was a large marble-topped, carved and gilded console table. Above it hung one of two large and elegantly gilt-framed mirrors. The other hung over the mantel.

All of this furniture arrived in the early fall, but the carpet ordered at the same time was not received until February. It was a large oval velvet Aubusson, made to a plan sent by President Monroe. The background was green "with a beautiful border, and in the centre the Arms of the United States of America colored. . . ."

The first floor Oval Reception Room seems to have kept the crimson and gold of the Monroe decorations for the next fifteen years, through John Quincy Adams and Andrew Jackson.

When Van Buren, in 1837, covered the chairs and sofas in blue, hung blue draperies at the windows and made the walls blue, the Oval Reception Room became known as the Elliptical Blue Salon. It is probable that this room has ever since been blue.

The Buchanan gilt furniture used in the Blue Room, 1857 to 1902, now in the Smithsonian Institution.

Courtesy Smithsonian Institution

18

Martha Patterson changed the walls from "paper of velvet and gold" to panels surrounded by "a rich border of black and gold." The furniture was recovered in patterned silk. Some mirrors were regilded and some "of rather ancient design" were replaced. At their reception that December no one saw the delicate new rug. Martha had covered it with muslin to keep it clean.

The old chandelier was converted to gas by President Polk.

Brown Brothers

The Blue Room in Johnson's Administration, 1865.

The circular settee, an object of conversation in America and abroad, was made to hold a plant to top the centerpiece. Buchanan's new greenhouse must have kept it well supplied.

From about 1850 not only the Blue Room but the other rooms in the White House (and homes throughout the nation as well) reflected the increasingly confused taste of the last half of the century. Empire Classicism gave way to Gothic and Italian Renaissance influences. All the elaborate styles of Europe followed and over-

The Blue Room in Cleveland's first term, about 1887, showing Arthur's robin's egg blue decorations.

Leet Brothers

The walls and ceiling are as Tiffany created them, "with ornaments in hand-pressed paper touched out in ivory, gradually deepening as the ceiling was approached." The rosettes set effectively with pieces of opaque and colored glass, the ceiling an elaborate interlacing of shields and stars.

The furniture is Buchanan's. The Hannibal clock, vases and standing candelabra are from Monroe.

Through the open door the famous stained glass screen in the hall is visible.

19

Courtesy President Benjamin Harrison Home

The Blue Room in Harrison's Administration.

lapped. People with newly made wealth felt a strong desire for display which the curved and heavily ornamented roccoco styles
satisfied. Furniture designs freely mixed unrelated ideas and motifs.
In the last two decades machine made, jig-sawed furniture, carved
and cheaply ornamented, became popular through the Centennial
Exposition in Philadelphia in 1876.

In the White House about every ten years rugs and carpets, uphol-

McKinley's Blue Room shows the trend to lighter decoration.

Leet Brothers

In his second administra-
tion Cleveland repainted
the Blue Room, still in
robin's egg blue. Whether
Cleveland or McKinley put
the pseudo Louis XVI pan-
els on the walls there can
be little doubt that the fil-
igreed valance (seen re-
flected in the mirror) is
Mrs. Harrison's.

20

The walls were covered with a heavy blue repp copied from a fabric used in the Petit Trianon and bordered with a Greek key motif in gold above the white wainscot. Windows were hung with the same material, with the same gold border, valances were formally draped from a gilded, eagle-topped cornice.

The mantel designed by architect Charles McKim was also copied from the Petit Trianon. Two matching bundles of arrows support the mantel shelf.

The Minerva clock had been used on the Blue Room mantel by Monroe and the candlesticks are from Monroe also.

Theodore Roosevelt returned the Blue Room to classic simplicity, 1902.

Detail of the arm-chair and stool, 1902.

The simple white and gold stools and armchairs, in the style of the First French Empire, and the caned and shield-back side chairs were covered with a fine blue lampas, patterned in gold. Specially woven, it was copied from an old French design of the Directoire period. Architect Stanford White used the entire design for chair backs and had the all-over background pattern woven for chair seats and stools.

Wilson reordered it when the house was being readied for his daughter Jessie's marriage.

stery and draperies needed renewing and walls needed fresh paint. Presidents were given the privilege of selling such furnishings as seemed to them unsuited or "decayed" adding the money from the sale to the amount allowed them by Congress. When they had little money for decorations, the White House became shabby and dirty; when they had more to spend the upkeep was better but often the rooms grew more ornate and cluttered. As a Reception Room, the Blue Room escaped much of the popular overcrowding.

In Grant's time the Oval Reception Room was sometimes called the Violet Blue Room for its warm, misty blue colors.

The most elaborate decoration of the Blue Room came in 1884 when Louis Tiffany created the robin's egg Blue Room for Arthur. Much admired at the time, its name and robin's egg blue color were carefully preserved through several Presidents' redecorations.

The Harrisons had changes made but the color in the fabrics and the paint was similar.

Cleveland, in his second Administration, repainted the Blue Room and, a contemporary said, again the robin's egg blue color.

In the last quarter of the 19th century, under the influence of outstanding American architects, "copying" period styles began to be fashionable. This trend brought many incongruous decorations but led to an appreciation of the simpler earlier styles.

In 1902, Theodore Roosevelt had the Blue Room shorn of its fussy decorations. Once more the graceful proportions and lines of the room were emphasized. His architects took much of their design for the Blue Room from 18th century French styles, contemporary with the building of the White House.

Photo Courtesy National Park Service

Deep blue repp was still used on the walls for draperies. It was also used for upholstery. The backs of both arm chairs and side chairs (which are no longer cane backed) were embroidered with the American Eagle and thirteen stars. The drapery valances were embroidered with stars and banded in the gold Greek key design.

Air conditioning units, though a boon in the Washington climate, did not improve the decoration.

The Blue Room in Franklin Roosevelt's Administration.

Thereafter there was little change in the decoration of the Blue Room for a half century.

In 1952 the Blue Room was carefully restored to its satisfying proportions and oval form. It remained the same charming reception room, seasoned through years of rich associations but given new luster and finish.

The fine polished floor of oak laid in a herring bone pattern was left bare. No carpeting has been used in the reception rooms since the 1902 restoration.

Courtesy F. Schumacher & Co.

←— *The 1952 Commission, grown conscious of the placing of the American Eagle, decided against its use on chair backs, and once more had the lustrous blue and gold lampas woven for the Blue Room. This time the urn and leaf motif was made, not only for arm chair backs but for the walls as well.*

The related all-over pattern was used for sidechairs and stools and also for the window hangings. The valances were draped much as they had been in 1902, from the same eagle topped cornice. The blue color was slightly lightened and brightened to give an interesting play of light and shadow on the walls and in the folds of drapery.

In the Truman restoration Monroe's candlesticks and the Minerva clock were used again on the white and gold mantel. The Waterford crystal sidelights were designed to go with the chandelier, a gift of several years ago. The fine blue Sevres vases in the windows replaced the disfiguring airconditioning units no longer needed. —→

22

The Blue Room in 1952.

Mrs. Monroe decreed that no President's wife should return calls. Caused much social wrangling at the time but the custom has been maintained.

Marie Monroe was the first daughter of a President to be married in the White House.

Criticism of Monroe for buying from foreign sources led Congress to pass act providing that "all furniture purchased for the use of the President's House be, as far as practicable, of American or domestic manufacture."

Monroe was reelected with only one negative vote cast as a token to reserve for Washington the only unanimous election.

There was probably no floor covering in the Oval Reception Room on January 1, 1818 when James and Elizabeth Monroe held the first formal reception in the White House, after it was rebuilt, since their oval rug did not arrive until two month later. The room was resplendent with their fashionable importations—glowing warmly with crimson and gold and the brilliance of crystal chandeliers. Against this elegant background Elizabeth Monroe set up a social order quite equal to that in diplomatic circles abroad. She was a gracious and dignified lady who had known the best in New York society as a girl, as well as diplomatic life abroad. She had neither the interest nor the strength to follow Dolley Madison's strenuous social example. With the support of Mrs. John Quincy Adams she at once established firm rules of precedence and custom.

Invitations for the Monroes' formal entertaining were sent to a carefully selected list, with meticulous regard for precedence. Many who had enjoyed the freedom of Thomas Jefferson's White House and Dolley Madison's expansive hospitality were displeased with what they felt was a regal attitude. They criticised the Monroes' social customs and their extravagances. There was much talk and lifted eyebrows over the solid gold service of spoons and forks they had brought from Paris. Gold table service was for kings. And eating with a fork was still frowned on as affected. Most Americans of that day ate with their knives.

For the better part of Monroe's first four years there was conflict among the socially elite. Mrs. Hayes, the Monroes' older daughter who assisted her mother, was headstrong and increased tension. The public was little concerned. After all, did not the Monroes open the White House one evening a week for anyone who wished to come and shake the President's hand? Even those who were annoyed with the Monroes for their "airs" were gratified by the high level of their entertainment. Early in the second term the fuss quieted down. Even the new precedence rules were accepted.

The North Front of the White House, 1825.

In 1818 an appropriation was made for grading and improving the President's "Square." A gardener was employed, grass was sown.

In 1825 John Quincy Adams succeeded James Monroe to the Presidency. The son of John and Abigail Adams, he was no stranger to the White House. His wife, Louisa Johnson Adams, was an unusually well-educated, intelligent woman who shared her husband's interest in national and international affairs. She was socially competent, schooled by her mother-in-law, Abigail Adams, and experienced in European society. While her husband was Secretary of State, the Adams household held a social position in Washington second only to that of the White House.

As President, John Quincy Adams was punctilious in matters of form and etiquette. He and Louisa continued the formal ways of the Monroes but less rigidly. Their entertaining was elegant and gracious. They invited people of all political opinions to share their hospitality; and Adams, feeling himself truly "the servant of the people," was always ready to see anyone who wanted to see him.

For himself he would have preferred the life of a country gentleman. He loved gardening and often took his exercise in the early mornings in the White House gardens. He improved the White House grounds with his fine plantings and made long-term plans for the gardens, some of which were carried out by later Presidents.

In his diary President Adams confessed that the round of constant entertainment bored him. He provides an amusing comparison of White House activities then and now. ". . . a large dinner party once a week, a Drawing Room once a fortnight. Occasional company of one, two or three to dine with the family, and the daily visitors, eight or ten, sometimes twelve or fifteen."

Today there are all the State and Diplomatic dinners and receptions and in addition to these functions representatives of organizations and many other groups to be received. During a typical season President Truman and his wife entertained 31,336 guests at official gatherings in the White House. They came in groups of a score or less to as many as 1,500. There were 86 overnight guests,

John Quincy Adams 1825-1829

Adams had been educated for statehood in Europe while his father was Minister. Later he himself had been our Minister in The Hague, Berlin, and London.

Beginning of political changes which were to end the theory of government by gentlemen.

One of five candidates in tangled election: none received majority. Congress elected Adams. His activities violently blocked by Jackson.

Opposed by Congress in foreign and domestic policies.

Established with his own funds Columbian University (now George Washington University).

Adams tried to get government to sponsor research in agriculture, science and the arts.

Tiber Creek came close to the White House as shown in this fanciful drawing.

Lafayette's "triumphal progress" through the country a high spot in Adams's administration.

exclusive of relatives, during the same period.

During office hours the President usually has from ten to fifteen official callers a day.

Tourists visiting the White House in 1948, until early November when it was closed for rebuilding, numbered 528,111.

No indoor swimming pool was needed in President John Quincy Adams's day. Then the Potomac River came almost to the White House grounds. Often President Adams, clad in his bathrobe, with a towel over his arm, walked down the path between the elder bushes to the river to start his orderly and well-filled day with an early morning swim.

Since James Monroe had taken back the furnishings of his own house it had been necessary to bring out of storage the makeshift pieces of the Madison's Octagon House days to add to the government owned French importations. Some of these showed wear from their years of use, although the Monroes had given them the best of care. And there were other rooms with no furniture at all.

The East Room

Adams was defeated after one term.

A year later he was elected to the House of Representatives and served seventeen years.

John Quincy Adams had long tried to get an appropriation for furnishing the East Room. At the same time James Hoban was urging Congress to provide money for the still unbuilt North Portico. A Senator, present one evening at a White House function in 1826, became distressed at the unfinished state of the East Room and persuaded Congress to allot funds to finish both the East Room and the North Portico. Adams finished the walls "in a fine lemon yellow" and left the rest of the East Room furnishing to his successor.

For a quarter of a century after the White House was first occupied the magnificent East Room was neglected. Misfortune, lack of funds and political jealousies contributed to delay. Even before the British burning, Latrobe wrote across an East Room plan that the ceiling had "given way." After the White House was rebuilt lack of funds still caused neglect.

When John Quincy Adams came to the White House interior details and finishing of the East Room were still to be done. It was largely used as a catch-all for broken-down and unwanted furniture, including a door screen, a washstand, a ewer and wash basin. Twenty-four mahogany chairs and four sofas intended for the room were stored there, partly upholstered.

However, on occasion the East Room was used by bringing in temporary furnishings. This was done for Marie Monroe's wedding reception and for Mrs. John Quincy Adams's fine ball, during their last winter. At other times the crowds, when receptions were large, "spilled over" into the unfinished Grand Reception Room.

In November, 1829, Andrew Jackson completed the decorations in the East Room. He put blue and yellow moreen at the windows

The East Room in 1859.

Although the East Room had been redecorated since Jackson's time the general plan of furnishing was still followed by Buchanan nearly 30 years later. There were still huge mirrors over pier tables between the windows and over the four great fireplaces. Pedestal tables were again placed under each of the large chandeliers.

against Adams's lemon yellow walls, and under them the usual fringed white muslin. At each window a gilded eagle held up the draperies.

The unfinished mahogany chairs and sofas were now made ready with covers of blue satin damask. The Brussels carpet, with a deep red border combined blues and yellows and pale fawn, pleasantly.

Jackson bought three resplendent chandeliers with hundreds of cutglass pendants in a new design. And under each he placed a fine, marble topped pedestal table.

Polite usage prompted Jackson's spending $12. for 20 spittoons.

Huge gilt mirrors hung above the four black marble mantels, their grates and brasses well polished. Bright fires, needed for heat, sparkled on the three chandeliers and rivaled the lights from their many candles, reflecting back in the eight mirrors.

A line of gilded stars outlined the cornice around the room and above the ornamental rays over the door was a semicircle of 24 stars.

In this magnificent room Jackson began the long continued custom of large receptions.

The East Room at the beginning of the Civil War.

The President and Mrs. Lincoln received in their elaborately curtained Grand Reception Room.

A contemporary wrote of Grant's redecoration of the East Room, "the style of the decoration is pure Greek. . . . The ceiling is divided in three panels. . . . the walls are raised paper gilded and painted in drab gray. The woodwork throughout . . . in white and gold." Great mirrors, 8 in all hang, as in Jackson's time, over mantels and between windows.

It was then that the ebony and old gold furniture and the "greenery yallery" carpet were new.

Bettmann Archiv

President Grant's reception for King Kalakaua of the Sandwich Islands.

Johnson's daughter used red brocatelle at the East Room windows to replace those cut up in the war years by the thoughtless souvenir-seeking public. There was a general freshening of paint and new crimson upholstery on the carved wood chairs and sofas.

From the attic she brought portraits of past Presidents for the walls. The floor was covered with a great Turkish rug, the gift of the Sultan, the warm color "giving to the room a comfortable air."

In 1873 Grant gave the East Room an entirely different face with false beams and great columns.

Then and for many years the over-ornate East Room was considered handsome. Arthur had Tiffany redecorate the ceiling only, although in his sweeping housecleaning he sold all of the East Room furniture and bought new. Mrs. Harrison used golden brown damask for draperies and furniture covers. The Clevelands painted, gilded, renewed varnishes and hung new lace undercurtains. But in 1900 it was basically the same.

In 1902, Theodore Roosevelt removed Grant's heavy structures from the East Room. With painstaking care, its interior was restored to the fine design of the late Georgian period. Its ornamentation was delicate and restrained. Twelve low relief panels were carved for the walls by the Piccirilli brothers. All the walls and woodwork were painted white. Simple marble mantels of a Georgian design replaced the former massive gold-and-white ones.

Three new crystal and bronze chandeliers hung from the ceiling, bronze electric light standards were placed in the corners of the room.

28

← *The architectural details are Grant's "pure Greek" white and gold. The ceiling is Tiffany's. Electricity was put in by the Harrisons.*

In 1902 McKim made a valuable structural change in the East Room. The projecting chimney breasts in effect divided the room into three bays. By setting them flush with the walls he gave the room its open and spacious appearance.

For his gold and white East Room Theodore Roosevelt used heavy yellow silk damask draperies at the window. The banquettes were covered with gold silk velours. There were candelabra on the mantel. There was a handsome new parquetry floor.

Underwood & Underwood

The East Room in the 1890's.

The East Room in Franklin Roosevelt's time.

The architectural details and the white walls have continued from Theodore Roosevelt's time unchanged, as have the chandeliers, the bronze standard lights and the furniture.

The Franklin Roosevelts used cranberry red silk for draperies, white walls, and gold in the furniture and fittings.

29

Franklin Roosevelt re-designed the legs of the brown mahogany piano into stylized gold eagles and planned the decoration showing folk dances of America.

The lemon gold and white damask (below) was especially woven for the East Room draperies from an 18th Century design. The fringe with which it is trimmed and the gold and white tie-backs were hand tied.

A lovely white and gold striped lampas (below) was woven to cover the gilded benches.

In the next fifty years freshening, new draperies, re-upholstery, new paint, were given when needed with superficial changes of color and fabrics. For the most part the room was satisfying.

Even in 1952 changes were slight. Some of the plaster ornamentation was modified to less romantic designs from the same period. The ceiling, especially, was too heavily ornamented not only aesthetically but for structural safety. New American motifs were carved in panels over the doorways—Indian heads, buffalo and both sides of the Great Seal of the United States. The Piccirilli panels were preserved. A handsome parquetry floor was relaid. Antique marble mantels of a soft brown red replaced those of the 1902 restoration.

In 1952 the East Room was decorated in white →
and gold. Against the oyster white walls a fine lemon gold and white silk damask was used for hangings. The valances were elaborately draped from the old regilded cornices.

Two priceless antique sofas, designed by Robert Adams and made by Chippendale, gifts to the White House, were placed under the portraits of George and Martha Washington. Their sapphire blue damask coverings are a striking accent.

The heavy chandeliers (each has 22,000 pendants) dating from 1902, were modified to improve their lines and lighten them for safety.

30

The East Room in 1952.

Andrew Jackson
1829-1837

Representative of frontier democracy.

Jackson was the first President to wear long trousers for formal occasions. Earlier Presidents wore knee breeches.

Introduced "spoils system." Over 1000 office holders replaced by his own supporters.

Generally ignored advice of his Cabinet Members and depended upon a small group of friends, called "the Kitchen Cabinet."

The magnolias Jackson planted on the White House grounds in memory of Rachel still grow and bloom there.

Water piped 1834.

Up to the time of Andrew Jackson the Presidents had all been landed gentry. "Old Hickory" was a man of the people, elected on a popular ticket and liked for his down-to-earth democracy. At sixty-one he was a colorful figure with a commanding personality. The kind of man to catch the fancy of the people. From an orphaned childhood he had grown to wealth and leadership. Rough and vigorous, he had wrested his success from the frontier. He was ruthless and determined toward an opponent, but with his family and his friends he was gentle, affectionate and wholly loyal.

With him to the White House came a new social order and a new kind of people. The doors were open to all. Thousands crowded in on his inaugural day to shake his hand—"high and low, old and young, Negroes and whites, poured in one solid column into this spacious mansion." They shouted, brawled, broke glasses, stood on the damask covered chairs and sofas to see their hero, and finally pressed so close that he escaped by the back way to his lodgings.

President Jackson's beloved wife Rachel had died just before his inauguration and he had brought his niece, Mrs. Emily Donelson, to be his hostess.

Although Jackson cared little for social life he continued the weekly Drawing Rooms and the big public receptions. These were announced in the newspapers and anyone might come. Refreshments were served and the people came in crowds. What the social life lacked in brilliance it made up for in attendance. But Jackson was not a stranger to fine living. He had made money and had learned to spend it. He especially liked to set a fine table and bought fine china and glass for the White House. His dinners were lavish. For his extravagances he spent his own money.

Jackson's last public reception was even more riotous than his first. He had been presented with an enormous cheese weighing 1,400

The South Portico and West Colonnades as they were built from Jefferson's plans. The South Portico was finished in 1824. The sketch was made in 1833.

pounds and, on Washington's Birthday at the end of his second term, he threw open the White House, inviting one and all to sample the cheese. The Senate adjourned for the day and hordes of people flocked in from all the surrounding country.

The great cheese was placed in the State Dining Room and the jam there was terrific as the crowd struggled for pieces of the cheese. A guest at the party wrote, "The scene in the dining room soon became as disagreeable as possible and I gladly left it." By day's end walls and silk covered furniture were smeared with cheese. Rooms and halls reeked of it. People said you could smell it blocks away.

It took weeks to clean up. Traces of the party were still there to distress Van Buren at his inauguration on March 4th of that year.

Martin Van Buren was also of the people, but his rise had been political. He had acquired for himself wealth and a taste for elegance. In the White House he began at once a thorough cleaning and re-doing, much of it unquestionably badly needed after the robust crowds of Jackson admirers.

He redecorated the East Room and made the first floor reception room blue for the first time—the Elliptical Blue Room. He bought new furniture, some for the bedrooms which had not been furnished since Monroe took his furniture home with him. For his own bedroom the President bought chintz bed hangings, and matching draperies at the windows were tied back with silk cords with tassels to show the fine muslin undercurtains. He bought quantities of china, glass and gold spoons.

Van Buren with his extravagant spending of public money especially angered the people because his elegance was reserved for a chosen few. He gave epicurean dinners. But the weekly Drawing Rooms were no longer held. The public was invited only once a

These iron pipes were the first of a long succession of improvements that almost destroyed the White House.

Before this time water for the White House was carried or pumped in wooden troughs. In John Adams's time it was carried 5 long city blocks from Franklin Park.

Martin Van Buren 1837-1841

Van Buren was the son of an innkeeper and a farmer, people of modest means.

Helped Jackson's election. Jackson's support made Van Buren's dream of being master of the Mansion come true.

The new nation's prosperity brought period of heavy spending and over-extended credit. Two months after Van Buren became President the depression hit and lasted five years.

The White House in 1848. From Pierce to Grant, D'Angers' statue of Jefferson stood before the White House.

Courtesy N. Y. Public Library

Van Buren served no refreshments at his annual open house reception on New Year's Day.

The depression made the people doubly resentful of Van Buren's luxury.

Van Buren was also given a huge cheese. He did not have a party but through a local store sold pieces of the cheese to the public and gave the proceeds to charity.

William Harrison
1841-1841

Elected as war hero under the slogan "Tippecanoe and Tyler too."

John Tyler
1841-1845

John Tyler insisted that the Vice President assumes the Presidency on the President's death. This precedent has since been followed.

Texas annexed to Union as a slave State.

James Knox Polk
1845-1849

Mexican War added almost as much territory as the Louisiana Purchase.

Northwest boundary dispute, compromised at 49th parallel.

year on New Year's Day. Nor were the people pleased with the sight of their President driving about in his handsome green coach with its green-liveried coachman.

Van Buren was a widower and when his eldest son married Dolley Madison's young relative, Angelica Singleton, she became hostess and brought to the White House not only the prestige of her class but an appetite for being regal which outshone Van Buren's. Angelica, wearing a purple velvet gown and a headdress of three feathers, received royally seated on a raised platform in the newly done Elliptical Blue Salon.

With all its new finery the White House was still underheated and badly drained. A contemporary writes, "Mr. Van Buren had the glass screen put across the windy entrance hall and great wood fires made a struggle against the chill of the house but it was so badly underdrained that in all long rains the floors of the kitchen and cellars were actually under water."

These health hazards were blamed (perhaps with truth) by the wife of William Harrison for his death after only one month in the White House. John Tyler had been put on the ticket with him solely to get the Southern vote. The Whigs had never dreamed of his inheriting the Presidency.

Tyler's wife's ill health, followed by her death, led to a very quiet social regime through his first two years. His son Robert was the President's secretary and Mrs. Robert Tyler acted as hostess. Young Mrs. Tyler was a beautiful woman and popular in Washington.

Not quite two years after his first wife's death (those who disliked him said it was too short a time) President Tyler met and married the attractive, young (people said too young) Julia Gardiner of New York. As First Lady, like Angelica Van Buren, Julia Tyler chose to surround herself with regal trappings, like her, she sat on a platform to receive, attended by twelve maids-of-honor, "six on each side and dressed all alike." Like her she wore an elaborate headdress "formed of bugles and resembling a crown."

The serious minded James Polk worked hard through his four years. His wife worked with him as his secretary—an unprecedented and rather shocking thing for a President's wife to do.

Sarah Polk was a well-born Southerner. The marks of her class were in her fine bearing, her elegance in dress and her dignified and reserved manner. She was brought up a Moravian and was deeply religious. She permitted no card playing, no dancing and no alcoholic drinking at official receptions. At these highly proper evening receptions the guests spent the time "solemnly promenading around the East Room in pairs" or, while the military band played tunes out of doors, "everybody walked in and out without restriction; the President perhaps strolling over the lawn amidst the company ready to shake hands with anyone."

In 1848 gas lights were installed in the White House. Because she so loved the beautiful chandeliers in the East Room when all the candles were lighted, Mrs. Polk delayed putting gas lights in that room until after her big reception. The guests were just assembled when the new installation failed and all the rooms were left in darkness except the East Room where the candles burned brightly. Mrs. Polk was much praised for her foresight!

Zachary Taylor, a soldier hero who lived up to his nickname of "Old Rough and Ready," did not want to be President. His wife Rachel, worn with her rugged life, wanted less to be First Lady. But when he was elected Rachel Taylor followed her husband to Washington though she was not strong and preferred to remain apart from the social life of the White House. She spent her days upstairs visiting with her family and her few intimates or smoking her corncob pipe and knitting, to pass the time. Their twenty-two year old daughter, Betty Bliss, acted as official hostess. She was a sweet, natural young woman and Washington people referred to her affectionately as "our Betty." A visiting nobleman wrote that she did the honors "with the artlessness of a rustic belle and the grace of a duchess."

Taylor was an agreeable man in manners and appearance, honest and hardworking but with no brilliance. He was little informed about political and national affairs and poorly prepared to take the Presidency especially when leadership was so desperately needed. Being a southerner and a slave holder his position was difficult. As President he owed allegiance to both the North and the South. What could he do? Could he just not take sides? Let Congress decide everything? It seemed the simplest way. But before his short sixteen months as President were over, Zachary Taylor had begun to realize that the President must take responsibility. No one ever knew whether he could have summoned the statemanship necessary to a good President because he suddenly became ill and died.

Vice President Millard Fillmore was thrown suddenly into the Presidency to face the monumental problems of the day. He was a methodical man. He introduced morning receptions and made it a rule not to work on Sundays, partly for religious reasons but more as a part of his well regulated plan for keeping well. He was a large man, well-built and erect, outstanding in a crowd. His manners were pleasant. He was well liked, but his administration was ineffectual.

By mid-century there were more and more advances in industry

Lowest tariff in U.S. history passed on principle of tariff for revenue only.

The Polks gave first Thanksgiving Dinner to be held in the White House.

Installation of gas 1848, one of first in city.

Zachary Taylor
1849-1850

On Sunday, March 4th, 1849, Polk's term had expired. Zachary Taylor refused to be sworn in on the Sabbath. The Presidency fell to the President of the Senate, David Atchison. Constitutionally he became President for a day. He said he was "dead tired" and slept through most of it!

Growing conflict over slavery.

Admission of California as a state.

Charges of corruption in his Cabinet decided him to reorganize his Executive Department.

Millard Fillmore
1850-1853

He signed the Compromise measures of 1850 including the Fugitive Slave Act. Trying to enforce it lost him his party's support.

Boston had for years had a law against taking baths except upon medical advice. In Philadelphia bathing was illegal between the months of November and February.

The old Negro cook had prepared "a fine state dinner for 36 people every Thursday in a huge fireplace with cranes, hooks, pots, pans, kettles and skillets."

Jefferson brought many of his own books to the White House. Some of these, which he sold to the Government, became the basis of the Library of Congress. They are there today. Other Presidents brought and took away with them their treasured books. But there had been no White House library.

At the White House the Fillmores enjoyed the music of Jenny Lind.

and invention. Fillmore made several innovations. His was the first bath tub in the White House. Gossips said he bathed regularly and elegantly in his tremendous zinc-lined mahogany tub.

Fillmore bought the first cooking stove to replace the laborious but picturesque method of cooking over open fires. Would you expect the cook to be grateful? Not at all. He found the new-fangled contraption strange and couldn't manage the draughts till the President showed him how.

At a Cabinet meeting in 1850 when the President and the Secretary of the Treasury disagreed about a word there was found to be no dictionary—nor even a library—in the White House.

Abigail Fillmore had been a teacher. In fact, she had guided her little schooled husband through four years of intensive study after their marriage. She knew and loved books and decided to do something about a library for the White House.

What could she do? Hadn't Dolley Madison said, "feed and flatter the men"? Abigail decided on a series of Congressional dinners. Such was her success that the funds were appropriated and Mrs. Fillmore was appointed to select the books.

Second Floor Oval Room

She set up her library in the charming second floor Oval Room which she had earlier made a family sitting room. When the straw carpet left by the Taylors was taken up she had found underneath a good Brussels carpet, with the old "basket-of-roses-upset" design. This she had cleaned. She sent for her own piano and her daughter's harp and furnished an attractive room. To it the books added their warmth and friendliness.

The Second Floor Oval Room, directly above the Blue Room was used by the John Adamses as their only reception room. When Jefferson finished the First Floor Oval Reception Room he kept the second floor room with its crimson and mahogany 18th century charm as a "Ladies Reception Room." During the years before the

The Second Floor Library-Sitting Room in Hayes's Administration.

The Hayeses liked to have friends in for informal music.

In his study Harrison used the old *Resolute* desk. This desk was made from the timbers of the S.S. Resolute. It was abandoned in a futile search for the British explorer Sir John Franklin and his party lost in Canadian waters, in 1852. Later it was salvaged and sent to Queen Victoria as a goodwill gift. When its usefulness was over, Queen Victoria had a desk made of it and gave it to the United States in Hayes's Administration. It has been used by many Presidents. In 1952 it was put in the Broadcasting Room.

The Second Floor Oval Room as Harrison's study, 1889.

upset of the "rule of gentlemen" it was most often a gracious private drawing room or music room. J. Q. Adams found there, remaining from Monroe's day, a "gilt mounted pianoforte, a dozen gilt chairs with satin covers and elegant figured satin window curtains." Adams added what was needed to make it a fine drawing room.

As need for more executive offices crowded the family, the room was increasingly often a family sitting room. Abraham Lincoln read from his Bible in this room which with Mrs. Fillmore's books had become a library-sitting-room, a character it kept for many years.

When Mrs. Harrison redecorated the White House she moved the President's study out of the Oval Room into the next room, now the Monroe Room, and often used as a President's study or as the Cabinet room. She made the Oval Room the family sitting room.

The Oval Sitting Room in Cleveland's second term.

This family room shows the vogue for pattern and overcrowding. The patent rocker was a popular innovation.

The Oval Sitting Room in the Hoover Administration.

The Hoovers furnished the Oval Sitting Room mostly with their own things. They brought with them their curved sofas, covered with black and gold brocade, the high painted Dutch cupboard, the many-drawered cabinets from South America, the black Coromandel screen and the piano.

The long high draped curtains in the south windows were lettuce green taffeta. Mrs. Hoover had the rug dyed black. Some of the chairs were covered with black velours and others with gray-green brocade.

She converted two unused doorways into charming shell-toped cupboards. (See picture bottom page 39.)

Harrison used it as his study for part of his first year but shortly moved into the room next (the Monroe room) and Mrs. Harrison took the Oval Room for the family.

Each family gave it a personal quality. Mrs. Taft brought teakwood furniture and oriental screens and made their sitting room reminiscent of the Philippines. Mrs. Wilson used chintzes, their well-loved books, paintings and sculpture to give it a home-like air.

In 1933 Franklin Roosevelt made the Second Floor Oval Room the President's study. Truman used it also. Before the House was closed for reconstruction he bought some furniture for it. A few new pieces were added and a specially woven fabric was used in 1952.

The Second Floor Oval Room was Franklin Roosevelt's study throughout his Presidency.

Franklin Roosevelt moved the Resolute desk into the Oval Sitting Room with its black rug and lettuce green taffeta draperies. Large leather lounge chairs from the East Hall Sitting Room were placed about the fireplace—some of them from Theodore Roosevelt's time. He added bookcases, extra tables and chairs. There were his old prints of the Hudson Valley and old ship prints, his ship models and many books to overflow the bookcases. His desk was filled with the trivia he always collected.

Photo by Abbie Rowe—Courtesy National Park Service

President Truman's Oval Study, 1952.

Courtesy Scalamandré Silks, Inc.

Detail of the President's Study, 1952, showing Mrs. Hoover's doorway-cupboards still in use.

For furniture and the window draperies a satin damask was woven in a lovely soft green patterned in gold. The design was adapted from an 18th Century fabric to suggest the seal of the President. →

In 1953, except that Eisenhower substituted his personal belongings for those of the former President, the study was not changed. Some of his decorations from foreign governments were placed here.

Franklin Pierce
1853-1857

Pierce a Northerner sympathetic to the South did little to solve national problems.

Gadsden Purchase added over 45,000 square miles to the Southwest.

By treaty Commodore Perry opened Japan to American trade in 1854.

In 1853, first heating system was installed.

James Buchanan
1857-1861

The mistakes made by Pierce and Buchanan increased the tensions between free and slave holding states. Buchanan was confused and ineffectual in the crisis.

With the election of Abraham Lincoln South Carolina seceded. Before the futile Buchanan had shut the doors of the White House behind him, six states had joined South Carolina to form the Confederate States of America, with Jefferson Davis as President.

Abraham Lincoln
1861-1865

Franklin Pierce and his wife were by nature quiet people. But the White House during his administration was more than normally quiet. On the journey to the Capital they had seen their only son —the last of three—killed in a railway accident in which they were unharmed. Mrs. Pierce held to the necessary social functions but with little heart.

Ambitious landscaping of the White House grounds was undertaken. On summer afternoons the people gathered to see the new beauty of the grounds and "to enjoy the music of the Marine Band and the pleasure of a fashionable promenade."

Shortly before Buchanan took office the greenhouses, the stables and the vegetable gardens at the east of the grounds were removed for an extension of the Treasury Building. The Commissioner of Public Buildings recommended building a new conservatory at the west of the House and removing the vegetable gardens from the grounds.

James Buchanan never married because of the untimely death of his fiancée when he was young. He brought his lovely young niece and ward, Harriet Lane, to the White House to be his official hostess. She had been with him when he was Minister to Great Britain and, although very young at the time, had learned much of diplomatic life. His Inaugural Ball was held, because of the crowds, in a temporary building in Judiciary Square. It was a gay and extravagant affair. The guests danced until four in the morning and consumed quantities of food. Harriet Lane's charm and fresh young beauty complemented the polished and distinguished manner of the handsome, white-haired President.

With the opening of the social season the following winter there was a succession of brilliant affairs. The House had been given a thorough renovation. The new conservatory, built on the west terrace, supplied fresh, fragrant flowers for all the rooms and grew the exquisite grapes which the gourmet Buchanan loved.

Queen Victoria's son, the Prince of Wales—later King Edward VII —was a Buchanan guest for five days. The White House staff had so increased that there was no available guest room. President Buchanan gave up his own room to the Prince and slept on a sofa in the hall. He also gave for him a magnificent banquet such as only Buchanan could devise. The Prince was delighted with his visit and Queen Victoria wrote her glowing appreciation.

Socially Buchanan was all that could be desired. But no one knew where he stood on the vital issue of the day.

Abraham Lincoln became President to a divided nation. His Inaugural Ball was, nevertheless, so large that, like Buchanan's, it had to be held in Judiciary Square. The White House was open to

The Lincoln Room, 1952.   Wide World Photos, Inc.

Lincoln's 7 foot bed and other furniture of his time were collected here where he signed the Emancipation Proclamation. Four chairs, like the one in the window, were used here when this was his Study and Cabinet Room.

the public and at Lincoln's first reception crowds of people came eager to see if the many rumors about the new President were true.

They found him as tall and as awkward as they had heard he was and as unpolished in appearance. But they sensed a sincerity in his simplicity and saw in his homely face a commanding dignity and warmth and kindliness. And those who came to know him enjoyed "his love of jest and anecdote . . . his tender pity for suffering and distress."

Mary Todd Lincoln had planned three large receptions to follow the Inaugural but within the month the State social life was cut off. The Civil War had begun. With the death of their second son, Willie, the saddened Lincolns entertained as little as possible. For the duration of war there were no big receptions except on New Year's Day.

Still the White House was crowded. Many people came and went. Shortly after the beginning of the war hundreds of troops were quartered in the elegant East Room. Cabinet members and statesmen came to confer with the President, office seekers and those who hoped for other material gain, men, women and children came begging clemency for their loved ones and the public, moved by hope or curiosity, thronged the White House.

In his study Lincoln worked late into the nights. Sometimes he could be seen, his tall form bowed in prayer over his desk or standing in the window looking off broodingly to the Virginia hills.

Not an abolitionist, but opposed slavery as an injustice, and fought its extension.

Civil War started April, 1861: ended April, 1865.

Emancipation Proclamation New Year's Day, 1863. All slaves held in states then in rebellion were declared free.

With the failures and successes of the War, Lincoln's political supporters deserted and returned. General Grant's successes in battle and General Sherman's occupation of Atlanta helped turn political opinion in his favor before the Presidential campaign of 1864 and he was re-elected.

41

His second inaugural address reflected his attitude toward the South and the spirit that would have directed his decisions in the years following the War. He closed his address:

"With malice toward none; with charity for all; with firmness in the right, as God gives us to see the right, let us strive on to finish the work we are in; to bind up the nation's wounds; to care for him who shall have borne the battle, and for his widow, and his orphan — to do all which may achieve and cherish a just and lasting peace among ourselves, and with all nations."

Other Presidents stayed at the Soldiers Home in summer to be near Washington but where the ground was higher and living more comfortable.

April 9th Surrender of Lee to Grant.

Andrew Johnson
1665-1869

A Southerner with Northern ideals.

Like Lincoln he insisted that the seceded States kept their standing as States.

Issued general pardon to all members of the Confederacy.

Immediately after his second New Year's Day Reception, 1863, Abraham Lincoln went to his study and signed the famous Emancipation Proclamation. A contemporary wrote:

"The roll containing the Emancipation Proclamation was taken to Mr. Lincoln at noon by Secretary Seward and his son Frederick. As it lay unrolled before him, Mr. Lincoln took a pen, dipped it in ink, moved his hand to the place for the signature, held it a moment and dropped the pen. After a little hesitation he again took up the pen and went through the same movement as before.

"Mr. Lincoln then turned to Mr. Seward and said: 'I have been shaking hands since nine o'clock this morning, and my right arm is almost paralyzed. If my name ever goes into history it will be for this act and my whole soul is in it. If my hand trembles when I sign the Proclamation, all who examine the document will say: "He hesitated."

"He then turned to the table, took up the pen again, and slowly, firmly wrote that 'Abraham Lincoln' with which the whole world is familiar."

Lincoln stayed in Washington during the long hot summers but moved his family each season a few miles away to the Soldier's Home. Each morning and evening he rode to and from the White House with cavalry escort. The President, wearing his usual black business clothes, rode beside his little son Tad on his small horse in a miniature copy of the uniform of the guard.

Mrs. Lincoln was a plump little person. She was ambitious, erratic and difficult, one moment pleasant and kindly, the next unreasonable and demanding. She was especially jealous of her own right of precedence and of her husband's gallantry to any other woman. Although she came from a good family she was touchingly unsure of herself socially and in matters of dress and most sensitive to gossip or slight. And because her family were Southern sympathizers many people unfairly questioned Mary Lincoln's loyalty to the Union. She showed increasing signs of mental unbalance, causing her overburdened husband great distress.

On the evening of April 11th the President and Mrs. Lincoln went to the theatre to celebrate the Union victory. During the performance Abraham Lincoln was shot by an assassin.

The grave responsibilities of the reconstruction period needed, perhaps as much as the war years had. the strength and vision of Abraham Lincoln. But Abraham Lincoln was dead. And it fell to Vice President Andrew Johnson to pick up the burden.

His wife, Eliza McCardle Johnson, was pleasant and gracious. She was invalided by consumption and, although interested in all the life of the White House, could have little active part in it. She continued to be, as she always had been, her husband's confidante and advisor.

Their household was large. Both their married daughters had come with their families. And their son, Robert, was his father's secretary. The five grandchildren and the President's fourteen year old son, Andrew Johnson Jr., made things lively. The tense, brusque President became relaxed and happy with his cheerful family.

Mrs. Martha Patterson, the elder daughter, was official White House hostess. She was admired for her industry and unassuming dignity. Her most absorbing hobby was the upkeep of the spotless "modern" dairy. She showed it to visitors with pride as Buchanan had shown his "grapery."

The war years had been hard on the White House. The carpets were worn and shabby; the fine upholstery on sagging furniture was ruined. A thorough housecleaning was needed. Mrs. Patterson personally supervised the renovation. With care and economy she made the White House fresh and livable.

During the wretched days of the impeachment trial Mrs. Johnson permitted no change or cancellation of official entertaining. She was calm and sure of her husband's acquittal. At the Diplomatic Receptions Martha Patterson and her sister continued to be poised and gracious.

President Johnson won his case by the narrow margin of one vote. His last reception was largely attended. The guests praised his social regime and gave belated approval of his policies. At the close of Johnson's administration on his trip home people cheered him at every stop, glad of his acquittal.

General Grant, made popular by his dramatic successes in the Union Army, was elected to the Presidency by a large majority. What did it matter that he knew little of politics? The people were tired of politicians. They packed the city at his inauguration.

Ulysses S. Grant was a kindly, sincere and trusting man. His own sincerity made him believe in the good intentions of his fellowmen.

The social life of the White House was growing in brilliance and elegance, not the courtly elegance of the early Presidents but with new manners, new wealth and much display and extravagance. Few of the old Southerners and more of the wealthy bankers and businessmen sat about Grant's luxurious table. There were places set for extra guests at every meal.

The President and Mrs. Grant broke precedence by going where they liked; and everyone came to them. They were so unassuming and natural that no one criticized them for it. Mrs. Grant was abreast of the affairs of the day and gave intelligent advice to her husband. She had always been accustomed to a social life, was friendly and a charming conversationalist. Their evening receptions were very popular.

There were gay young parties, too, for their lovely debutante daughter, Nellie. She was popular in Washington society and in Europe, where she travelled with family friends and became a center

Opposed giving equal civil rights to Negroes believing they were not ready for them.

A costly and destructive fire in the conservatory ruined many rare plants including a sago palm, prized "because it had been imported by George Washington."

Alaska bought in 1867 for $7,200,000.

Congress, trying to regain its power, opposed Johnson at every turn. Was angered by his independence, brought impeachment proceedings and even accused him of complicity in the death of Lincoln.

Ulysses S. Grant 1869-1877

Country on wave of expansion. Big manufacturers and capitalists growing in power and influence in affairs of state.

Prosperity contrasted with debt-ridden farmers and underpaid Northern factory hands.

Money was recklessly invested, fostering fraud and corruption and panics in both administrations.

Grant allowed himself to be duped in attempted "corner on gold."

Transcontinental railroads started. Railroad frauds.

of attraction. Nellie's magnificent wedding in the White House (to a young man she met on the boat) was the high point in the social life of the Grant Administration.

When Prince Arthur, the nineteen year old son of Queen Victoria, visited Washington, the President invited him, as he would any other distinguished guest, to the regular State dinner at the White House. Ordinarily the cost of these dinners ran between $100 and $300. But on this occasion Grant's Italian chef outdid himself. The dinner, exclusive of wines, cost $1500!

A report of the Commissioner on the condition of the White House led to an appropriation for renovation at the beginning of Grant's second term.

Not enough structural work was done to correct the basic problems. However, the East Room ceiling at least must have been safer with the massive beams and columns he put in that room.

The outside of the White House was unchanged from its Georgian style, but inside Grant had a mid-Victorian holiday. The rooms were given heavy over-ornamented architectural details and clumsy furniture, lambrequins draped from mantels and much gilding everywhere. It was all very "elegant" and quite in keeping with the taste of the time.

The Red Room

In Grant's second term the Red Room was elaborately decorated in what was curiously called an "English version of Queen Anne." Over the mantel as the principal wall decoration was a life sized painting of President Grant and his family. The gilt framed needlework firescreen, gift of the Austrian Commission, was there and two

Harrison's Red Room—"homelike with flowering plants."

Courtesy President Benjamin Harrison Home

The Red Room, 1902.

Theodore Roosevelt brought one of the pair of old white marble mantels from the enlarged State Dining Room, made the woodwork simple again, and covered the walls with specially woven rich red velvet. Furniture was upholstered in red damask.

The standard candelabra and the mantel vases are Monroe.

The vogue for hanging many pictures had not died nor had the popularity for fringe trimmed chairs.

In Coolidge's redecoration, the walls and draperies were red damask. Rugs for the Red and Green Rooms were ordered to match their wall colors, each with the seal of the United States as a central motif. The Red Room seal rug was put in the Library when this room was redone in 1935.

small Japanese cabinets, gifts of the Japanese Minister. The family used this room largely as a parlor.

Except for the earliest years when it had been the President's antechamber the Red Room has been a small drawing room used by the President's wife for her receptions and teas. Guests often gather there before going in to dinner. The Red and Green Rooms fill the need for smaller and more comfortably furnished drawing rooms for less formal entertaining.

It was called the "Yellow Room" in J. Q. Adams's time for the yellow beige hangings and carpet although the upholstery was crim-

Photo Courtesy National Park Service

Franklin Roosevelt's Red Room.

Light crimson damask was again used on the walls and for draperies in 1935. A new plain rug replaced the seal rug. Most of the furniture was covered in light red damask, a few pieces in gold colored damask, to harmonize with T. Roosevelt's gilded bronze chandelier. With the gilded cornices and mirror frames and Monroe's gilded standard candelabra and gilded vases the effect was charmingly crimson and gold.

Mrs. Grant's brass clock is on the mantel.

Wide World Photos,

The Red Room, 1952.

In 1952 a fine red silk damask was woven from an old design for the walls and draperies. The 1850 sofa, a gift, was covered with it also. White damask on the wing chair and on several Hepplewhite arm chairs, with the white of the woodwork, the marble mantel and the white silk casement curtains, serves as a foil for the red.

There is a new red chenille rug.

son. And because the full length painting of George Washington hung over the mantel for many years it became known as the Washington Room.

Theodore Roosevelt used red Genoese velvet on its walls and painted the woodwork white to match the white marble mantel from the State Dining Room. The Coolidges used red damask for walls and hangings and in 1952 again red damask walls and draperies were used contrasting strikingly with white woodwork and upholstery.

46

President Rutherford Hayes and his wife Lucy were well educated and high minded. Mrs. Hayes dressed well but with extreme simplicity. She received guests every evening at entirely informal gatherings that pleased the people. At the beginning of each day there was morning worship. And on Sunday evenings hymn singing was shared with Cabinet members and Congressmen, among them William McKinley

During their first holiday season in the White House, on December 30th, the Hayeses celebrated their silver wedding. With old friends and the minister who had officiated, they re-enacted their ceremony. On New Year's Day the public were received.

Mrs. Hayes's early decision to serve no alcoholic beverages in the White House earned for her the nickname of "Lemonade Lucy." She was much praised by the W.C.T.U. Later, they gave her portrait to the government as a tribute to her "leadership in family life on a high level of morals and dignity."

The Hayeses did not redecorate the White House on a large scale but they freshened it and made it more cheerful. They bought new wardrobes and sideboards to ease their storage problems. They installed the first telephone and the first telegraph. And they disposed of Fillmore's cumbersome bath tub and installed two bathrooms with running water.

By his determined stand on Civil Service reform President Hayes removed any possibility that his party would consider him for re-election.

The Green Room

Early Presidents used the Green Room as the Common Dining Room. But James Monroe furnished it as an elegant sitting room, with handsome glass and gilt chandeliers, mirrors and vases. He and his friends played cards there and it was known as the Card Room. The chairs were green covered and the draperies green silk over white dimity.

The Green color and name continued. In Jackson's time a writer refers to the Green Room as "odious to the ladies from the sallow looks it imparts." It continued to be used, as the Red Room was, for small social occasions and family gatherings.

After the Civil War Mrs. Patterson made the Green Room "cozy and homelike" with Lincoln's rosewood and ebony furniture covered with green and gold brocatelle which was also looped back over lace curtains at the window.

Arthur found the furniture worn and moth-eaten and sold it all. With his new furniture he hung new green silk curtains over white fringed muslin against a silver wall.

Roosevelt covered the walls with green Genoese velvet, and Presidents since have used fabric on the walls.

The election was so heavily contested that the electoral commission came to their decision only two days before his inauguration. Mr. and Mrs. Hayes were on their way to Washington before they knew certainly that they were to live in the White House.

An able and efficient executive.

Withdrew the Federal occupation troops from Louisiana and South Carolina.

Urged civil service reforms to stop graft.

Temperance was becoming popular at this time. Many people preferred that the White House set an example by serving no spirits. General Grant had served coffee instead of liquor at one of his large receptions.

He attacked Chester Arthur, who held a civil service position in New York City, for his political connections.

The Green Room in Cleveland's first term.

The portrait of Mrs. Hayes hung over the piano from the close of the Hayes Administration, when it was given, until 1902. It now hangs in the corridor of the ground floor.

The vases beside the fireplace were the gifts of the Chinese Ambassador in Arthur's time.

Mrs. Harrison redecorated the room "tastefully" in pale green with plain paneled walls, a plain carpet and plain green plush covered chairs. Hers was the first marked trend away from the overuse of pattern. Electricity was added to the gasolier.

In 1902 the Green Room walls and draperies were of a specially woven velvet, in green, with white painted woodwork. Roosevelt found a marble console, of the same early date as the marble mantel, which he brought into this room. The Chinese vases are still beside the mantel, and on it the Hannibal clock and the vases from Monroe. Here, as in the Red Room, many pictures were hung.

The old gasolier was replaced with a new crystal electrified chandelier. →

The Coolidges used a soft green damask for walls and draperies, with similar color on the furniture. The first of the seal rugs used in this room was ordered by the Coolidges at this time. The room was furnished in antique pieces given by anonymous givers, the first fruit of Mrs. Coolidge's plan. The crystal chandelier was also given then but was not installed until Hoover's time.

Mrs. Coolidge was given enough antique furniture to furnish the Green Room, including the lovely Waterford chandelier which was not hung until Hoover's time.

In 1952 the cornice of the Green Room kept the original Hoban design but the ceilings in the Red, Green and Blue Rooms were lowered to one height, making space for the air-conditioning ducts. This banished the F. Roosevelt's disfiguring air-conditioning units and was thought to improve the room's proportions.

The Green Room, 1952.

Wide World Photos, Inc.

In 1947 shortly before the White House was closed the Trumans redecorated the Green Room. The seal rug grown shabby, was copied. The green brightened to an emerald to match the color of the new damask walls and draperies.

These were carefully stored during the restoration and reused in 1952. The furniture was recovered, some in green damask and some in lemon gold and green. Two fine Adams chairs were added to the antique furnishings.

James A. Garfield
1881-1881

In making appoint-
ments, he by-passed the
"Stalwarts" who had re-
luctantly supported his
election.

Garfield's young son,
Irving, is said to have
coasted at full speed
down the grand stairway
of the White House on
his high-wheeled bicycle,
turning spectacularly at
the bottom and sweeping
into the East Room, "the
flashing spokes of his
wheel vanishing like the
tail of a comet."

Garfield was shot by
a disappointed office
seeker July 22nd.

Chester A. Arthur
1881-1885

Most unpopular for
connections with scan-
dalous "Stalwarts," his
social position and
wealth.

Put only qualified men
in office and backed civil
service reform of 1883.
Gained public confi-
dence but lost him sup-
port of his politicians.

James A. Garfield won the next election in a campaign stressing his log cabin birth, for its sure-fire appeal to voters. He was actually a gentleman of excellent education who had served for a long time in Congress. His charming, alert mother, "Grandma Garfield," came to live in the White House and delighted Washington. The old lady, who had split fence rails in her pioneer girlhood, was unimpressed by the elegance of White House parties. "Law," she said, "I would rather do a good day's washing."

Garfield, a buoyant, light hearted man, loved to romp with his sons on the White House lawns. The old house had a warm family air in the short four months the Garfields were there. A visitor saw their young son, Irving, coasting at full speed down the grand stairway on his high-wheeled bicycle, turning spectacularly at the bottom and sweeping into the East Room, "the flashing spokes of his wheel vanishing like the tails of a comet."

Had President Garfield and his wife, Lucretia, carried out their intentions they might have stopped the tide of garish decoration in the White House twenty years earlier. Within their first month they went to the Library of Congress to find out what they could of the House's history to guide their planning. Material was scarce, even as it is now, and their progress slow. Time for such pursuits was short. Garfield quarrelled bitterly with his party over his Cabinet appointments which he insisted on making purely on a basis of merit. The politicians claimed the offices as their rightful reward. Vice President Arthur sided with the party and against the President.

Before these matters were settled, in July of that year, a political maniac fatally shot Garfield.

For nearly two months Garfield fought courageously to live. Through those hot weeks the political and social life of Washington waited. Vice President Arthur was sent for but was given no active duty until Garfield died, September 19th.

Chester Arthur, the handsome, fastidious widower was appalled at the condition of the White House. He refused to live there until Congress appropriated money enough to permit him to make the house fit to live in, by his standards.

In the full scale housecleaning that followed, Arthur removed and sold at auction 24 wagon loads of household effects. These included all the furniture from the East Room and the Green Room which was badly worn and broken and part of the furniture of the Red Room in a similar condition. Carpets, mantels, window hangings, chandeliers, beds, anything which seemed unsuited to President Arthur; Jackson's furniture, and a partly eaten suit of Lincoln's, and a rat trap that caught the rat that ate the suit that belonged to Mr. Lincoln.

The North Entrance Hall in Arthur's time.

Tiffany's opalescent glass screen in the hall which reached from the floor to the ceiling and had a motif of eagles and flags interlaced in the "Arabian method," served to keep off drafts and give privacy to the State Rooms. Panels "magically" opened here and there, as hidden doors. The floor was multicolored tiles.

The Harrisons elaborately frescoed ceiling and panels over the mantels in terra cotta and gilt. The much admired screen and tiled floor were kept until 1902.

Photo Courtesy National Park Service

Arthur brought the well known New York decorator, Louis Tiffany, to take charge of his decorations. All the important rooms were given the Tiffany touch, in the height of fashion. It was now that the Blue Room became robin's egg and the Red Room was given its elaborate friezes and gold ceiling.

The North Entrance Hall

The Georgian simplicity of the North Entrance Hall was retained until 1884. Then Tiffany climaxed his decorations with his multi-

Like the other widower Presidents, Jefferson and Van Buren, Arthur took careful interest in the slightest detail of the renovation of the White House.

Arthur's was not the first glass screen in the Entrance Hall. Before there was a heating system, even roaring fires offered little resistance to the cold.

In 1837 Van Buren put up a screen there, probably of clear glass, and in spite of the new heating system in Grant's time, he replaced the glass screen, which was removed on social occasions.

⟵ *The North Entrance door.*

Tiffany set stained glass panels into the front door.

Courtesy President Benjamin Harrison Home

The Entrance Hall about 1913.

Much as it looked in 1902 when Theodore Roosevelt removed the Tiffany screen and replaced it with six rising marble columns. A new floor of Joliet stone was laid, and the walls and ceilings were replastered with simple classic details. The bright colors were changed to buff and white. Floor to ceiling mirrors replaced the mantels and the decorative panels over them. Curtains and the long Corridor rug were in deep crimson. Bronze standards for electric lights and a new bronze lantern brightened the Hall.

Directly beneath the lantern the President's Seal, with the dates 1792-1902, in yellow bronze, was inlaid into the stone floor.

colored magnificent hall. It was restored in 1902 to its classic design; the colors were subdued to soft buff and white.

In 1952 its architecture was basically unchanged—except for the more dramatic treatment of the main stairway. The six stately columns of white marble veined in celedon and the delicate hint of green in the off white walls gave new beauty.

Stairway to the Second Floor, 1902.

When T. Roosevelt removed the family staircase for additional space in the State Dining Room, he put the new stairs to the second floor at the east end of the corridor just left of the East Room door, across from the Green Room.

The stairs were of Joliet marble and the gates wrought iron.

52

Photo by Abbie Rowe—Courtesy National Park Service

The Corridor adjoining the State Rooms, 1952.

Truman's Presidential Seal in color is over the door. The red chenille rug in the Corridor and the red damask draperies were new shortly before the renovation and were used again.

The bronze standard lights are from Theodore Roosevelt.

Most of the architectural detail from 1902 was restored.

The niches are from the original, more interesting, Hoban design which was uncovered when those made in 1902 were removed.

← *View of Corridor looking toward the East Room.*

Wide World Photos, Inc.

The Family Dining Room in Cleveland's first term. In the 1880's nothing about the gas-lit Family Dining Room suggested it could ever have been Georgian. Lavishly carved mahogany furniture, the draped mantel and trivia made it cozy. Some of the little heart-backed chairs later found their way about the House and in 1952 are still found here and there.

In the 1890's, although still much patterned, the designs became less bold. The furniture was the same until 1902.

Arthur's was an elegant administration. The White House got its first elevator, and Arthur, who was known for his impeccable dress, had the first White House valet. His sister, Mrs. McElroy, lived at the White House as official hostess, but the entertaining was cut to her brother's extravagant pattern.

The Family Dining Room

He preferred perfect small dinners in the private dining room with its walls newly papered in rich gold and the windows hung with "pomegranate velours." Twenty people could be seated there. Sumptuous dinners prepared by his exceptional French chef were served them. There were always corsages for the ladies and boutonnieres for the men.

This room, at first the State Dining Room, has for almost a century and a half been the President's family dining room.

Descriptions of elaborate floral arrangements for White House dinners, receptions and weddings make no mention of palms until Arthur's State Dinner, January 20, 1884. From then on they are mentioned continually.

The Family Dining Room in Franklin Roosevelt's time.

Little changed from the 1902 restoration, the cove ceiling, the plaster ornamentation and the mirror (copied from an old one in Boston of the early Federal period), are from Theodore Roosevelt's time.

The fine mahogany chairs and table have remained there since they were given to Mrs. Coolidge.

In Franklin Roosevelt's time the draperies and rug were red against the white walls and woodwork.

Wide World Photos, Inc.

The Family Dining Room in 1952. Removal of air-conditioning units and the more formal treatment of the red damask draperies added greater dignity to this charming room. The walls and woodwork were restored as they had been since 1902. The same fine old furniture was used. Its

Grover Cleveland was welcomed warmly by the outgoing President Arthur. Cleveland's openly expressed opinion, so flattering to Arthur, that, by not renominating him, the Republicans had missed their best candidate, served as a bond between them. President Arthur and his sister gave an Inauguration Day luncheon for President Cleveland and his sister. Their friendship was immediate, warm and lasting.

To assist at his first State reception, Cleveland invited Mrs. Folsom, widow of his best friend and early law partner, and her daughter Frances. Frances's father had been killed in an accident when she was eleven. Cleveland had been named in his will as her guardian. He had watched over her as she grew up and had helped to guide her through her education.

During this visit President Cleveland proposed marriage to his ward. But the habit of fatherly advice was so strong that at the same time he urged her to go to Europe with her mother for a year and think over her answer. Within six months Frances was back with her Paris trousseau ready. They were married in the Blue Room before a group of about forty people—the only marriage of a President in the White House.

Cleveland had bought a house in Georgetown where, as he wrote his sister, he could "be away from this cursed constant grind." Except for the social season when they must be in the White House the Clevelands lived there. The White House was given a much needed house cleaning while they were away—a coat of white paint outside, upstairs rooms painted, State rooms freshened.

Grover Cleveland had two terms but with the inconstancy of politics Benjamin Harrison's four-year term came between.

Benjamin Harrison was a dignified, aristocratic man who had held public office capably. But he lacked understanding of the unrest and problems of this new day.

The Harrisons were a large four-generation family—Mrs. Harrison's father, their married daughter and her husband, their married son and his wife and Mrs. Harrison's niece. The household was circumspect but lively. They revived the custom of morning prayers. There was gaiety, too, and children's play. And there was dancing once more in the White House.

The President worked hard but took time for long walks and drives with his family and a game of billiards with friends. Mrs. Harrison was fond of literature and expressed her artistic talent in her hobby of china painting. She liked the conservatory and took great pleasure in growing orchids. Never were the floral decorations at the White House more beautiful.

Her large family made Mrs. Harrison especially aware of the in-

Grover Cleveland
1885-1889

There were other bonds. The bachelor Cleveland and his sister, who was to be his hostess, and the widower Arthur and his hostess sister were all ministers' children.

He supported the civil service commission.

Replaced only "offensively partisan" Republicans in office.

He vigorously fought graft.

Opposed free coinage of silver.

Urged lower tariff for relief to farmers, but Congress changed bill to be almost useless.

Lost party's support and reelection.

Benjamin Harrison
1889-1893

Grandson of President William Harrison.

Supported his Republican party's high tariff.

Disability Pension Acts of 1890 and progressive civil service reform.

Held first Pan-American Conference.

McKinley Tariff Bill established commercial reciprocity agreements.

If the President's family were large someone had to sleep out to make room for an overnight guest.

Electricity put into the White House in 1893.

Mrs. Harrison ordered new china, 1500 pieces, each of a different design, showing the flora and fauna of America.

Through her interest in china Mrs. Harrison started the collection of Presidential china which continues and is displayed in the China Room.

Grover Cleveland 1893-1897

The Panic of 1893.

Chicago World's Fair.

Cleveland's second child, the only President's child born in the White House.

William McKinley 1897-1901

McKinley opposed war with Spain.
Assistant Secretary of Navy, Theodore Roosevelt, urged action.
Sinking of the *Maine*, Feb. 15, 1898, McKinley yielded to aroused public opinion.

Spanish American War won in 100 days: treaty, Dec. 10, 1898. Oc-

conveniences and crowding in the White House. She had the architect Fred D. Owen draw up three plans. One called for a separate private residence for the President in a new location and the other two were for fantastically elaborate enlargements and additions. Congress did not approve her plans but they made an appropriation for renovation and redecoration. Mrs. Harrison at once cleaned up the ground floor, cleared out the rats and took up the rotting and slimy old floor. At this time they put electricity in the White House, one of the earliest installations in the city. And the old hot water heating system was replaced with steam. There was much fresh paint, new upholstery and hangings. The Tiffany screen still dominated the entrance hall and part of the other Tiffany decorations remained in the State rooms. Many of the family rooms were completely redone. There was a new use of pale green and the flower colors Mrs. Harrison loved. She was praised for her "refined and artistic taste."

In the fall of the last year of Harrison's term his wife died of cancer. With other personal sorrows and political rough sailing, Harrison was glad to return the mantle of responsibility to Grover Cleveland.

Cleveland had sold his house in Georgetown Heights when he left Washington four years earlier. He now rented an estate in the same section and once more took his wife and their new little daughter to live there.

Cleveland was operated on that summer for cancer of the mouth which he kept secret believing it would be politically disturbing. But under the strain his austere personality grew more unbending. His second administration had become increasingly difficult with problems of graft. Against these he made determined and bold stands.

Ordinarily many guests would have been invited to the Inauguration Eve dinner given by the Clevelands to the President-Elect but because Mrs. McKinley was epileptic they invited only the McKinleys. At the last, Mrs. McKinley was unable to come. The incoming and the outgoing Presidents eagerly took the opportunity to discuss alone the serious problems of the nation, with great satisfaction to both.

In spite of her malady Mrs. McKinley went everywhere with her husband. He was unusually devoted and considerate of her. They held only the routine social functions and, except when completely unable, Mrs. McKinley attended all State dinners and receptions.

Plans were nearly completed for the Buffalo Exposition to mark the hundred years of progress. McKinley felt this would be a proper time to enlarge and improve the White House. For more than fifty years there had been constant complaints. No longer was it the dig-

58

nified and suitable President's House of Hoban's plan. Commissioners warned of rotting timbers, unsafe ceilings and dangers to health in the lack of sanitation. When many people were expected it had become routine to put shores under the floors of the East Room and the State Dining Room for safety. And temporary runways were always built to move the guests in and out.

With more executive work to be done in the White House the already cramped family living was further crowded. If the President's family were large some one had to sleep out to make room for an overnight guest. The West Wing, built to help take care of offices, had been buried under the conservatory and its rooms used for potting plants and other work of the greenhouses. The East Wing, removed in Grant's time, had never been rebuilt. This meant that all the services and storage formerly in the wings had been crowded back into the main building.

Sums of money had been spent on improvements but mostly for paint and decoration.

Everyone agreed something should be done. But what? Colonel Bingham, Superintendent of Public Buildings, came up with an elaborate model based on one of Mrs. Harrison's plans.

Horrified at the possibility the American Institute of Architects countered with the proposal that the White House be restored to Hoban's intention. There was general agreement.

Before much was done, six months after his second inauguration, William McKinley was assassinated while attending the Pan-American Exposition in Buffalo.

Theodore Roosevelt was singularly prepared to cope with the problems which faced him. Born to wealth and position, he had seen public service, was a statesman, a soldier, and a natural leader. He knew first hand many sections of the country. And he saw clearly that the changing times called for change in the national conduct of affairs.

Theodore Roosevelt gave his hearty support to the restoration of the White House. He was appalled at the dilapidated, dreary rooms filled with bric-a-brac, bead-fringed lampshades, clumsy furniture, gilt and shiny varnish and the endless meaningless designs.

cupied Cuba with promise of independence. Took Puerto Rico and Guam as reparation. Bought for $20,000,000 Philippines, with promise to liberate.

Hawaiian Islands annexed.

Annexations of new territory gave U.S. greater prestige and her Ministers were raised to rank of Ambassadors.

Boxer Rebellion. Cleveland forced western powers to guarantee territorial integrity of China.

Put U.S. on a gold standard.

Theodore Roosevelt 1901-1909

At 43, youngest man to become President.

Roosevelt's reforms were many.

Sherman Anti-Trust Act.

The White House, 1901.

The greenhouses had grown bit by bit to completely cover the West Terraces.

59

Urged "open door" policy in China.

Mediated to end Russo-Japanese War.

Supported The Hague Tribunal.

Meat Inspection and Pure Food and Drugs Acts.

Panama Canal begun.

Jefferson built his office here where Theodore Roosevelt put the Executi Building in 1902.

With characteristic energy Roosevelt got things moving as soon as Congress made the appropriation. Work was started in early June to be finished by November. On the President's orders construction and State rooms came first. The date for finishing was kept and so was the budget.

McMillan Commission set up to restore the city to L'Enfant's plan and the White House to Hoban's.

From old prints and plans which they found in the Library of Congress they restored the East and West Wings to their former usefulness. At the west they added a one story building for executive offices to separate business and living. Theodore Roosevelt's plan which re-established the President's House as a residence for the President's family was one of the most important and far-reaching results of the 1902 restoration.

1952. Southwest view of the West Executive Building showing the raised ro and the sunken court, by which it was enlarged by F. Roosevelt in 1935.

There are now 59 Executive Departments, committees and special offices set up by law to serve under the President and report to him directly. These number about 1500 persons who have offices in the West and East Wings and in the Old State Department and other nearby buildings.

East Entrance 1902. Box trees on the park-like promenade above the porte-ochere.

The porte-cochere could shelter 500 people. New circular drive permitted three carriages to approach at one time.

They built a porte-cochere which, with the East Wing Colonnade, sheltered guests to the entrance of the main building on the ground floor. They built necessary coat rooms in the East Wing.

Under the East Room dressing rooms for distinguished guests were built. They had toilet facilities for the first time.

Formerly the butcher and baker had driven grandly up to the North Portico and had lugged supplies down area steps to the storerooms and kitchen. A new driveway was built at the lower level so that deliveries could go under the Portico without coming into view.

The old iron balustrade at the north entrance was replaced with stone. The jutting bracket lanterns, which broke the fine line of the columns, were also taken down and, instead, a single lantern was hung from the ceiling of the Portico.

The old foundations for the East Wing were found during the digging.

Electrical wiring and a new heating plant, not planned for, had to be done at a cost of $13,000. Work on the private rooms was cut down by that amount.

1952. East Wing as it was enlarged during F. Roosevelt's time.

Photo Courtesy National Park Service

In 1942 Franklin Roosevelt had the East Wing enlarged for needed office space. A bomb shelter was also built. The interior of the East Entrance Hall was not completed then. Water pipes and electric ducts, exposed on walls and ceiling, and raw cement floors were left.

It was not until the fall of 1953 in Eisenhower's Administration that the walls were paneled in birch from floor to ceiling and the floors laid in Vermont marble.

The Ground Floor Corridor, 1902, graced with Hoban's vaulted arches and restored to usefulness.

The portrait is of Mrs. Theodore Roosevelt.

The new heating system was laid in trenches over which new stone floors were laid.

Because the land sloped to the south, the ground floor had full windows on the down side. With the East and West Wings to take care of storage and utilities again, these areas were returned to use as public rooms. The heavy heating apparatus was removed from the ceilings of the corridor and the new heating system was sunk in trenches overlaid with new stone floors. The 15 foot wide corridor was not only a spacious passageway, dignified by Hoban's vaulted ceiling, but when furnished it became a comfortable sitting area. A new stairway led from the corridor to the attic.

The terraces, (160 feet by 35 feet each) were furnished with boxwood, trees, fountains and garden furniture.

At the south, now that the sprawling greenhouses were gone, the East and West Wings with their lovely Colonnades again gave balance to the House.

The terraces over the colonnades were reached on the east from the East Room and on the west from the newly enlarged State Dining Room.

1943, showing Hoban's long flanking Colonnades and the locations of the East and West Wings as Franklin Roose enlarged them.

As in Arthur's time, the Harrisons used "glowing yellow" in the State Dining Room, harmonizing with Monroe's famous gold centerpiece shown here.

The white marble mantels ordered by Hoban for the rebuilding were used in the State Dining Room from 1818 to 1902.

The sur tout de table is made up of sections of mirror surrounded by a band heavily ornamented with fruits and flowers. Sixteen figurines spaced about it hold in their outstretched hands crowns in which cups may be put as holders for candles or small flowers. With it are used elaborate gold candelabra, baskets and tripods.

The filagree valance is similar to that Mrs. Harrison used in the Blue Room.

Electricity was put in the gasolier at this time.

Courtesy President Benjamin Harrison Home

The Harrison's State Dining Room.

Gold candlestick and basket from the Monroe table pieces.

The State Dining Room

The enlargement of the State Dining Room in 1902 was the only major change in any important room from Hoban's original plan. (This was still true in 1952.) Before the British burning, this room had been used as the Cabinet Room. The Monroes furnished it for State dining with fine mahogany tables and 36 haircloth covered mahogany chairs from their home. They hung "handsome fringed" draperies, laid a green and brown Brussels carpet, and entertained lavishly at dinners served from their imported china with silver and gold plate. Their 13½ foot centerpiece is justly famous and has continued in use. Thirty-six people could be seated for State dinners; perhaps enough in the days when meals were prepared over open fires. As social needs grew, sometimes tables were set up in the corridors for larger crowds, and sometimes the East Room was used, as Hoban had intended, as a Banqueting Hall.

In 1873 Mrs. Patterson used neutral tinted walls and carpet in the State Dining Room with green satin damask for draperies. She bought two new "modern sideboards." From the passage beyond, a flight of steps led to the greenhouses and grapery. Artificial flowers were items of considerable cost for use on the tables in Jackson's day and for other Presidents before the greenhouses were built. From Buchanan's time on fresh flowers were used profusely in table decoration. Many Presidents especially those whose lavish table was their pride—Buchanan, Grant and Arthur among them—used corsages and boutonnieres as well.

The State Dining Room in 1904.

The new carved mantel in T. Roosevelt's time came in for a good bit of attention. Roosevelt disapproved the lion heads McKim had carved in the new large mantel for the State Dining Room. So keenly did he feel that the animals should represent America that before he left the White House, at great expense to himself, he had buffalo heads carved to replace them.

Hoover hung the picture of Abraham Lincoln where it has since remained.

Theodore Roosevelt removed the stairway from the hall between the State and Family Dining Rooms and extended the State Dining Room to include that area. This made it possible to seat 100 people.

The walls were beautifully paneled in oak. Although the design is Georgian, the effect of the decorations—with the Flemish tapestries, the animal heads, trophies which Roosevelt wished displayed there, and arm chairs in 17th century style—was English Renaissance.

The natural oak paneling was preserved by the succeeding Presidents. After the trophies of the hunt and the tapestries were removed its Georgian character could be seen.

In 1952 the paneled walls were taken down with utmost care and replaced exactly as they had been. The wood was painted a soft light green in keeping with the Federal tradition.

Franklin Roosevelt also made an addition to the fireplace. He had John Adams's prayer for the White House carved across its panel, where it remained until the mantel was removed in 1952. (See page 96.)

The Franklin Roosevelts kept the natural wood color of the paneled walls. The draperies and chair seats were green velvet and the carpet a soft green, which was pleasant with the natural color of the wood panels.

Photo by Abbie Rowe—Courtesy National Park Service

In 1952 a new green chenille rug was bought to harmonize with the soft green walls and the deep green of the simple Vermont marble mantel. The gold silk damask draperies, new before the restoration, and the gold velvet on the chair seats were a pleasant contrast. Theodore Roosevelt's silver chandelier was gilded to go with the carved gold frame of the old English overmantel and candlesticks.

← *North wall of the State Dining Room showing the gold framed mirror and flower painting which, with the pair of rare English candlesticks, form the overmantel, gift of King George VI of England.*

The State Dining Room, 1952. The fine 18th Century table was a recent gift, the chairs an earlier one.

← The Kitchen in 1893. Theodore Roosevelt made few changes in the kitchen, some conveniences and needed refrigeration rooms were added.

The old kitchen with — the vaulted ceiling was for many years a lost room used solely for storage. In 1952 it was reclaimed to usefulness again. The great fireplaces at either end were restored to their original design, from old stones upon which the first White House artisans had carved their initials and the emblems of Masonic orders. The cranes are the original ones used in the preparation of countless Presidential dinners.

The Kitchen

For the better part of a century the kitchen was a large brick-floored room with arched ceiling and two huge stone fireplaces where before the first cook stove, all Presidential meals were prepared. Some time before 1900 the kitchen was moved to the northwest corner and the old kitchen became a neglected storeroom. The Franklin Roosevelts in 1936 installed an all electric kitchen. In 1952 it became a model of efficiency in stainless steel, monel metal, glass tiles, with the newest modern electric equipment.

Roosevelt used the room next to the Oval Sitting Room as his office. He had a door cut through so he could be with his wife between evening appointments.

There were two new suites of bedrooms and baths over the East Room with new furnishings. In the family sitting room (now the President's Study) nothing was done but the repairs and repainting needed because of the re-wiring. In Roosevelt's Study (now the Monroe Room) simple book shelves were built and plain buckram covered the walls. The rest of the second floor rooms were given new hangings and furniture covers only.

Theodore Roosevelt's bedroom.

The old Lincoln bed and many of the pieces of furniture now in the Lincoln Room were in the President's bedroom at that time.

66

he ancient kitchen in 1952 became a broadcasting room as efficient as a Broadway studio.   Wide World Photos, Inc.

The Roosevelts, with their six children were a happy and very active family. Edith Carow Roosevelt had grown up in the same New York social set as her husband. With the assurance of their breeding they lived without ostentation. They preferred to serve most of their meals in the family dining room. Mrs. Roosevelt had a special top made for the table to be able to seat their large family and still have room for distinguished guests. Often the baby sat in his highchair with them.

The children attended the public schools and indiscriminately brought home to the White House the friends they had made. They collected a "menagerie" of animals and walked on stilts all over the mansion. The President often joined their wild and hilarious play at the end of the day.

Alice Roosevelt's debut, the day after their first New Year's Reception in the White House, was a delightful dancing party. She was very popular and much in the limelight. The newspapers found her "good copy" and avidly followed her adventures, including her trip to the Orient with the Taft Commission, her presentation to the imperial families in China and Japan, and the romance that started on shipboard with Nicholas Longworth, to whom she was married in the White House in 1906.

This "found" room was fully wired with outlets in the ceiling for both sight and sound, for broadcasting by radio and television. Color and monotone receivers were built into the President's Study and the West Hall Sitting Room on the second floor.

The Broadcasting Room was furnished with comfortable chairs covered in tapestry and in leather. The old Resolute desk is shown in front of the fireplace. Draperies were made of silk and linen damask in mustard gold.

Alice was as spirited and full of energy as her father. He had taught her to enjoy ju-jitsu, riding, dancing, walking—

all the forms of exercise that, through the encouragement of his own father, had changed his sickly childhood to vigor and vitality.

Roosevelt gave away his niece, Eleanor, when she married Franklin Roosevelt.

Roosevelt decided not to try for another term and gave his support to Taft who, he believed, would carry on his work.

William H. Taft
1909-1913

Taft would have preferred a seat on the bench of the Supreme Court to being President. He was appointed Supreme Court Justice later.

Continued many of Roosevelt's policies. More vigorous fight against big trusts.

Taft believed government appointments to be a matter of high trust. He made his appointments for merit only. Disappointed office seekers and losing job holders made him politically unpopular. Began the rift

There were many distinguished visitors, among them Prince Henry of Prussia, brother of the German Emperor. Theodore Roosevelt gave a large dinner for him at which only gentlemen were present. The banquet was set at a great crescent-shaped table in the East Room and the decorations featured thousands of tiny red, white and blue electric lights in the shapes of stars, anchors, ropes and other such symbols, from a canopy of smilax.

The Roosevelts held strictly to precedence and etiquette but in a gracious and effortless manner. After large receptions, they often held private supper parties for special guests set at little tables in the second floor corridor. Their musicales, held most Friday nights during the summer, were considered the President's wife's parties. Mrs. Roosevelt received alone in the Red Room. The guests passed on into the East Room. Here just before the music began the President brought in their dinner guests. Punch and ices were served afterward.

To reduce the profligate waste of the country's natural resources, Roosevelt invited all the State Governors, members of his Cabinet, the Chief Justices, and key men in science, politics and education to a three day conference in the East Room where huge charts and maps covered the walls. As a result many States established Conservation Commissions and an educational program was started to show the important relation between the nation's resources and its welfare.

When William Howard Taft became President he was already well known in official Washington. He was a large, dignified and kindly man, fair and conscientious. Both the President and Mrs. Taft liked people and liked entertaining. They kept the traditions in their official entertaining, but they were easy and friendly and saw no reason why they should not go to dine and lunch with their friends.

Their household reflected their warmth and love of family. They employed a housekeeper instead of a chef. And the President bought the first White House car—an electric brougham.

The three Taft children tusseled and romped happily through the House. The story is told that their favorite fun was to slide on large tin trays down the grand staircase, ending at the bottom with a great clatter. Discarding dignity, White House aides and other grown-ups joined in. "Many distinguished personages have bumped joyously down the long flight of marble stairs."

In spite of his size Taft liked to dance and was "light on his feet." And Mrs. Taft with the aides and a few friends formed a dancing class for exercise and recreation.

There was dancing, too, at the debut of their daughter, Helen. Panes and frames were removed from the doors and windows to arrange a musicians' balcony for the Marine Band on the terrace outside the East Room. It freed the entire floor for the dance.

The Tafts held delightful musicales. The greatest artists came to perform knowing they would have intelligent appreciation.

Mrs. Taft had loved the life in the Philippines and she brought to Washington, in addition to her teakwood and oriental screens, the pleasant custom of greeting friends on fine evenings in Potomac Park. The plan was based on the Lunetta in Manila. All Washington enjoyed walking about or driving in carriages, greeting friends and being seen. President Taft came on his great black horse and often invited a senator to ride with him.

Because of Mrs. Taft springtime in Washington has come to mean cherry blossom time to thousands of visitors.

Taft was personally liked, but ineffectual. He was nominated again but Theodore Roosevelt and his "Bull Moose" Progressive party split the Republican vote and the Democrats won the election.

Woodrow Wilson was a new kind of man to be President—not a soldier hero nor a politician but an educator and a student of government.

He was a tall, proper-looking man who combined stubborn self-reliance with a love of fun and charm. Ellen Axon Wilson and their three young daughters were devoted to him. In the pleasant Oval Sitting Room the family often listened while the President read aloud or they held long discussions or became hilarious at his clowning. The fun-loving Wilson girls, so the story goes, joined, incognito, a sight-seeing trip around Washington, ending up with a tour of the White House, and no one the wiser.

The eldest daughter Margaret was a trained social worker and was also working seriously toward a singing career. The two younger daughters Jessie and Eleanor were engaged and both married in the White House. There were more than the usual number of gay young parties with three young daughters in the household.

Mrs. Wilson was not well and, in the second August of her husband's first term, she died.

A little more than a year after his wife's death Woodrow Wilson married again. The second Mrs. Wilson like the first was a devoted wife. She was a very attractive woman, poised and well-dressed.

When the war, which Wilson had tried so hard to avoid, came, the White House became the center for its conduct and the President worked night after night. For Wilson who hated war its only justification was in "a war to end war" and a treaty which would mean lasting peace.

The White House joined the nation in Herbert Hoover's "wheatless" and "meatless" days and on "gasless" days drove the old Victoria

between Taft and Roosevelt whose friendship later broke completely.

Enlarged Executive Wing.

High tariffs had become an issue with both parties. Taft's administration failed to lower them.

Through her the Municipality of Tokyo gave the city of Washington some 3000 cherry trees.

T. Woodrow Wilson 1913-1921

Tariff revised down.

Federal Reserve Act, helped by Farm Loan Act, sought to control capital.

World War I began April 2, 1917. Germans sank *Lusitania* and *Sussex,* endangered all shipping.

Wilson's mediation between the warring countries failed.

Germany's renewal of unrestricted submarine warfare led to Wilson's declaration of war and rapid mobilization of nation.

Wilson attended the Versailles Conference, Spring, 1919. The peace treaty, including the plan for the League of Nations, was attacked by isolationists and never ratified by the Senate.

At the war's end he quickly lost his popularity and Congress gained an opposing Republican majority.

18th Amendment, 1919, prohibition.

19th Amendment, 1920, women's suffrage.

Reconstruction period difficult with problems of demobilized soldiers, wounded veterans, industrial upset, etc.

Warren G. Harding
1921-1923

Separate peace treaty with Germany signed.

Scandals in Veteran's Bureau and in Departments of Justice and the Interior early in Harding's administration led to exposures that mark it as one of the most corrupt in U.S. history.

War officially declared ended July 2, 1921.

The Ohioan Harding started the custom of inviting friends for breakfast of pancakes and maple syrup (Ohio variety); Vermonter Coolidge continued it with maple syrup (Vermont variety).

to church. And Mrs. Wilson learned to ride a bicycle in the long ground floor corridor. They had an extensive "war garden," as well.

The President and his wife visited canteens and embarkation centers to cheer the men who were going overseas. Margaret toured America singing in the camps and later went to Europe to sing for the soldiers the simple songs they loved.

In his eagerness to insure his peace plan Wilson went to Europe. When he returned it was rejected by his Republican Senate. So Wilson decided to go directly to the people with it, not only in scheduled appearances in the large cities but at every whistle stop in the country. Before he could finish the trip the strain had become too great for him. He collapsed and was brought home.

During the entire remainder of his term (more than a year and a half) Wilson continued to direct the affairs of the Nation from his bed. Mrs. Wilson was constantly with him, guarding his limited strength.

Wilson looked forward to the next election, hoping that another Democratic President with a supporting Democratic Congress would pass his plan. But the people voted for the promised "normalcy" and isolation.

The White House had been quiet and closed to the public all through the war years and Wilson's illness. With the Hardings it was again brightly lighted and gay.

Warren Harding, a tall, well built man, was genial and easy, "one of the gang." Being neither particularly ambitious nor eager for overwork he cut down the routines of his office to a few hours a day to have time for the things he enjoyed—golf, poker and the company of friends. The running of the nation he left largely to his Cabinet. His Cabinet was made up of a few honorable, conscientious men, among men whose dishonesty led to their disgrace and dismissal.

Mrs. Harding, who was far from well, was ambitious for her husband and she was energetic and vivacious as a hostess. She originated huge garden parties at the White House for sick and wounded veterans. From the White House greenhouses she herself selected and made up little bouquets of flowers and took them to the men whom she visited at Walter Reed Hospital.

No wines were served on the White House table because of National Prohibition but "drinks" were served at the President's private poker parties.

By the second spring of his term there were rumors of waste and fraud and disgraceful oil scandals. The talk included the President.

His political advisers hoped a personal appearance might win back some of his support and sent Harding across the country and to Alaska. On the return journey he died in California.

Few people knew much about the silent, retiring man who inherited the Presidency. Calvin Coolidge was not involved in the scandals of the Harding administration. The public felt safe with the shrewd, honest Vermonter.

Grace Coolidge was a pretty woman whose friendliness and gaiety put everyone at ease. Her smiling, outgoing personality did much to make her husband's Administration successful, but she had no part in the political world.

The Coolidges had always lived simply. They remained unpretentious and sincere, and Mrs. Coolidge, who thoroughly enjoyed the White House, blossomed there. She considered her opportunity to entertain and meet all kinds of people a rare privilege. She liked to talk with the many visitors to the White House and often photographed an interesting looking person or a small child.

The death of their second son from a foot infection while home on holiday saddened the Coolidge Administrations.

The Queen of Rumania was entertained at the White House by the Coolidges. The President's disapproval of the handsome Queen's publicity plans was characteristically silent and firm. The Prince of Wales (later the Duke of Windsor) was another of their guests.

It became essential to support the White House roof. While it was being rebuilt with new steel girders Coolidge had the roof raised, inconspicuously, so that another story could be added. They installed new bedrooms and baths on the top floor and a sewing room and storage rooms. Mrs. Coolidge's "Sky Parlor"—a room with three glass walls, comfortable chairs and a view—gave sanctuary and much pleasure to the Coolidges and to later Presidents and their families.

President Coolidge chose for his study the room Lincoln had used. Mrs. Coolidge found in the warehouses a chair said to have belonged to Andrew Jackson, and to have been used also by Abraham Lincoln. She put it in her husband's study. In further search she found only one or two tables of any interest but she was inspired by a plan. She suggested that Americans who owned fine pieces would like to give them to the White House to become a part of a living collection. Congress agreed and passed a resolution making possible the acceptance of such pieces from "anonymous donors." In Coolidge's Administration enough antique furniture was given to furnish the Green Room and the valuable table and Chippendale chairs for the Private Dining Room. By 1952 there were many gifts— among them the choice and rare Adams sofas used in the East Room, the beautiful chandelier in the Private Dining Room and the fine 18th Century table for the State Dining Room.

Calvin Coolidge had a quiet humor. He was amused by the "legend" he had become and often slyly gave it a bit of assistance.

In the next elections Calvin Coolidge did not "choose to run."

Generally little legislative activity.

Favored governmental economy, reduced national debt and taxes.

Exceptional prosperity during his first term brought credit to him. The country voted to keep him in office at the next election.

1948 this weight on the unsupported second floor was found to add greatly to hazards of collapse.

Mrs. Coolidge herself crocheted a bedspread for the Lincoln Bed. This is now in the Smithsonian Institution.

Although he served 7½ years he had only one elected term.

The Sun Room, 1952, an enlarged octagonal version of Mrs. Coolidge's "Sky Parlor," provides privacy and relaxe for the President's family.

Furnished in bamboo and refreshingly cool colors, the Sun Room opens onto a roof promenade. Chairs from the Harrison's State Dining Room were placed about a table of 18th Century design where informal meals are sometimes served.

← *The contemporary chintz is a jack-in-the-pulpit design with green and blue flowers and a gray fern background, harmonious with the large blue glass areas and the bamboo of the furniture.*

72

The Rose Room, 1952, is done in delicate tones of the color that gave it its name.

This most important guest room is sometimes called the Queen's Room because four queens have slept there: Queen Wilhemina of the Netherlands, Queen Marie of Rumania, Queen Elizabeth of England and Queen Juliana of the Netherlands. (Elizabeth II of England also slept there as Princess.)

The draperies are a pale rose taffeta with pink and blue tasseled edging. There is a pale rose in the hangings of the beautiful Chippendale bed (a recent gift) and in the covers on the fireside chairs. The rug is soft blue.

The copy of Mrs. Monroe's chest is near the window.

An adaptation of a lovely old Italian design woven in a textured silk damask was used on several chairs. →

James Monroe signed his message to Congress, which contained the Monroe Doctrine, on this Louis XVI desk. Made of mahogany, it is heavily bound with brass, and the corner columns are inlaid with fluted brass strips. The top, surrounded by a brass rail, is of Vermont marble which was, oddly enough, imported by France.

The armchair was always used with the desk. Mrs. Hoover had both carefully copied for the White House.

Herbert C. Hoover
1929-1933

As Secretary of Commerce, Hoover gave new purpose to that department.

The Executive Wing of the White House was burned in 1929 and was modestly rebuilt by Hoover.

Herbert Hoover followed Coolidge. He was already internationally known for his distinguished and efficient public works. During the war his name was a household word all over America because of his food saving program.

The Hoovers were widely travelled, wealthy, philanthropic. They liked informality, were most hospitable and lavish in their entertainment. There were always extra unexpected guests. At State Receptions they urged Cabinet members to mingle with the other guests instead of remaining in the Blue Room as had been the custom.

They held charming musicales. Mrs. Hoover had fifty armchairs made with handsome carved gilt frames, upholstered in rich silk brocade. These replaced the little gilt chairs usually used and, although fewer could be invited, Mrs. Hoover had the satisfaction of knowing that her guests were as comfortably seated as the Hoovers.

Lou Henry Hoover was lovely, tall, whitehaired and exceptionally gracious. Among her many activities the Girl Scout organization remained dear to her. Often there were meetings of its national officers at the White House or at the Hoovers' Rapidan Camp.

When they came to the White House the private rooms were not well furnished. Mrs. Hoover, who had a great interest and talent for arrangement and decoration, made many pleasant improvements. She made the long second floor corridor look lived in and friendly, with comfortable chairs and white bookcases filled with books. There were rugs here from South America and objects of interest and beauty from the Hoovers' travels all over the world. House guests usually waited here to go down to dinner with their host when dinner was informal.

The west end of this corridor called the West Hall Sitting Room was always used by Presidents' families. Mrs. Hoover had the deep fan-topped window screened to make an aviary for canaries, with a dry tree to perch on and plenty of room to fly and sing. On the checkerboard grass rug she arranged wicker furniture. Ferns and blossoming plants in long copper trays bordered the palm-lined walls making it a pleasant indoor garden for relaxation.

The East Hall end was furnished as a man's sitting room with great leather chairs and sofas. On the walls hung Mrs. Hoover's framed collection of pictures of the White House—from reproductions of the original architects' drawings to contemporary engravings.

President Hoover used the Lincoln Study. The *Resolute* desk, flanked by the two official flags, was set near the window. Over the mantel was a picture of Lincoln's Cabinet by which Mrs. Hoover identified the "Lincoln chairs." She had seen these Victorian chairs with the Gothic trefoil piercing scattered through the house. She had them renovated and brought to this room where they are now. Here, too, Mrs. Hoover hung a little mirror which was looted in 1814 by a British soldier and now returned to the White House.

The books were a gift of the American Booksellers Association. One of its members had discovered at the Hoover Inauguration that the White House had no books. Each year new volumes are added to the collection. (No one seems to know what became of Abigail Fillmore's White House Library.)

Mrs. Monroe's Louis XVI chest is a companion to the President's desk made of the same wood, brass and marble. Mrs. Monroe used a little round, brass-galleried, marble-topped tea table to match. The chest, the tea table and the footstool shown here and the little candlestand pictured on page 17, were also among Mrs. Hoover's replicas.

Mrs. Monroe's portrait and new gift of hanging shelves are Monroe copies.

From early American chintz, Metropolitan seum of Art.

The Monroe Room, 1952, showing Mrs. Hoover's copy of the Monroe desk. The portrait over the mantel is James Monroe

The history of the White House furnishings so interested Mrs. Hoover that she had research and records made. She gathered into the room (which had been Mrs. Monroe's private parlor) at the left of the Oval Sitting Room a few pieces which had belonged to the White House in the Monroe period—a charming Empire table from France, two sofas made in Alexandria and two arm chairs, a group of occasional chairs, a gilt wall mirror and on the mantel a pair of Sevres vases. When she learned that original furniture used by the Monroes in the White House was displayed in the James Monroe law offices in Fredericksburg, Virginia, she went to see it.

The beautiful furniture inspired her to have faithful copies made for her "Monroe Room," and the copies were exquisitely done. There was the desk where the Monroe Doctrine was signed and the chair used with it, a chest of drawers, Mrs. Monroe's tea table, a card table, a dainty pedestal table and a fine copy of the painting of Mrs. Monroe which had hung in the White House in that Administration. The piano was too difficult to copy but an identical one was given for the room. The Hoovers used the Monroe Room as a delightful private Drawing Room.

In the Franklin Roosevelt administration Mrs. Roosevelt moved the Monroe furniture to other rooms. She made of this room a conference and press room for her busy public life.

The Trumans made the room a drawing room again and with the Rose Bedroom and the Lincoln Room it formed part of the suite for distinguished guests.

In the fall of the Hoovers' first year there were beginnings of the economic collapse which increased through the Administration. Herbert Hoover worked ceaselessly to try to stem its tide. The Hoovers did not leave Washington except for week-ends at their Rapidan Camp in the Virginia Mountains.

Hoover's experiments in relief made little headway. By the end of his first term the depression was in full flood. To the people his long term plans for a sound economic system seemed too remote. They turned hopefully toward the promises of the New Deal.

Franklin D. Roosevelt quickly took drastic action to fight the depression. He had watched from the sidelines the effects of Hoover's measures. He could see why some failed. Some with promise he promoted. With the help of a cooperating Congress he pushed through many revolutionary plans under the banner of the New Deal. Not all were successful nor socially desirable. But it was a time for taking bold steps and Franklin Roosevelt, like his late kinsman Theodore Roosevelt, was courageous and resourceful.

Almost at once he began his "Fireside Chats" to the nation. His manner was assured and his magnetic voice, carrying to them his

Stock market crashes and general business depression began the fall of Hoover's first year.

Appointed many commissions to study national problems, conferred with business leaders on procedures to keep a normal economic activity.

Called special session of Congress to enact the Farm Relief Act and establish the Federal Farm Board.

Public works were advanced to relieve unemployment.

He created, 1932, the Reconstruction Finance Corporation.

Congress passed an Emergency Relief Act and created the Federal Home Loan Banks.

Franklin D. Roosevelt 1933-1945

Elected by a great majority.

Declared a bank holiday, second day in office.

With a Democratic majority in both houses of Congress he had great power for leadership and used it.

Went off the gold standard Hoover had tried so hard to save.

Started vast program of public works to relieve critical unemployment.

The Tennessee Valley Authority typifies his land reclamation program.

Rural electrification.

Prohibition abolished 1933.

Social legislation included old age pensions, unemployment insurance, slum clearance and other housing projects, abolition of child labor.

Panic past by 1935.

Lend Lease Program.

Broadcast Proclamation of March 27, 1941, calling on Americans to face the vital need to defeat Hitler, a "virtual declaration of war."

Atlantic Charter established August 1941.

Pearl Harbor, Dec. 7, 1941. U.S. entered World War II.

plans and encouragement, won him the support of the people. His knack for phrase-making made them remember what he said.

Roosevelt, although an aristocrat of wealth and social position, had a firm belief in the rights of the common man. About ten years before he became President, his promising political career was interrupted by an attack of poliomyelitis, so severe that he never again stood without the aid of braces and canes. He gained understanding during the years of his illness. His wife, Anna Eleanor, had for years been active in social reforms and politics. She brought many people to his bedside to discuss their problems and help him keep his interests alive.

Mrs. Roosevelt went to the White House a bit regretfully. To a woman with her keen mind and capacities and interests the duties of a White House hostess looked dull. But when the President sent her to the Appalachian Mountains to report to him first hand the conditions there her enthusiasm was aroused. That was only the beginning. Eleanor Roosevelt went everywhere the President could not go and brought back to him the human story behind every reform or bill. He highly valued her opinions and abilities.

She was the most active First Lady in the White House. So widespread were her interests that it is unlikely that those of any other will surpass or even equal them. She thought nothing of a conference in Washington in the morning, flying to New York for luncheon and home again in time to receive with her husband at a State Reception. She was, at the same time, devoted to her large family and managed to be on hand when one of them wanted her. There were dozens of parties and dances for the young people. Sunday night suppers, with Mrs. Roosevelt scrambling eggs in a chafing dish, were a family institution. In her spare times she wrote for the papers and magazines and gave radio broadcasts. And she always carried a bit of knitting for her own grandchildren or other people's babies.

Official entertaining was unusually heavy and the Roosevelts added more receptions to be able to get everyone in. They put no undue importance on rank and entertained dignitaries with the ease and friendliness they would show a neighbor. In the war years White House meals were kept carefully within the rationed limits.

The Roosevelts moved into the White House with very little fuss.

Both were more concerned with people than things. Mrs. Roosevelt shifted the furniture, hung her husband's prints. The Oval Room became the President's Study. His adjoining bedroom was convenient. Here he used a simple iron bed and a minimum of entirely utilitarian furniture: a bureau, a white painted bedside table, an old rocking chair and the essential heavy old wardrobe. It was exactly to his taste.

The Roosevelts fitted up the west hall sitting area with a tea table, comfortable sofas and chairs, gay with red and white. Mrs. Roosevelt hung the walls generously with prints from her husband's collection. Between palms, in the large fan window, was a table, on it a framed photograph of the President. In this homelike room family breakfasts and intimate dinners were often served. Here the family met daily for tea. And here each year on Christmas Eve in the glow of their taper-lighted Christmas tree the President read Dickens's Christmas Carol aloud.

The Executive Offices in the West Wing were enlarged by raising the roof inconspicuously for another floor, much as it had been done earlier to the White House, and by extending under ground areas with offices around a sunken court.

An addition was built on the East Wing offices after World War II had started and a bomb cellar was included.

Again war made the White House the citadel of the Commander-in-Chief of the armed forces. On the ground floor Roosevelt set up a map room. Here were charted all the strategic moves of the Combined Chiefs of Staff, representing all the Allied Armies. Winston Churchill was often here. Soldiers guarded the White House doors, machine guns armed its roof, and blackout curtains at the windows concealed its lights.

Shortly after he was elected President for the fourth time and only a few months before the end of the war, Franklin Roosevelt, with shocking suddenness, died.

Harry Truman stepped modestly into the Presidency. It was not easy to be expected to fill the vacancy of a man whose hold on the nation had won for him a fourth election. And it was awesome to take leadership in the midst of a great world war. Harry Truman had not the generations of wealth and position behind him to make him feel "born to rule," nor had he, yet, the confidence that comes from the people's vote. But he was experienced in politics and he had a humble and sincere desire to do the right thing for the nation.

Almost at once the new President was faced with a soul stirring decision. Should he use the atom bomb? He knew what horror and devastation it was capable of. He knew that without it the lives of American and allied soldiers would continue to be sacrificed to a long drawn out and cruel war. In his own words it was "an almost unbearable burden, [the] responsibility of deciding whether to use this weapon for the first time."

His decision brought VJ Day and the end of combat. Over night the world moved into the Atomic Age. There were all the usual problems of government, appointments, budgets, price control and over all the vital questions of control of the atom bomb.

America had become a world power and Washington a world

When King George and Queen Elizabeth visited them, the Roosevelts entertained with ceremony at the White House. But on the week-end in their home at Hyde Park they gave a large informal picnic and delighted the royal pair by serving "hot dogs."

His third term election broke a precedent established by George Washington. He was given a fourth term which his death cut short at its beginning. Immediately after his death Congress adopted a Constitutional Amendment which does not permit any future President to seek a third term.

Harry S. Truman
1945-1953

Less than one month after he took office V.E. Day ended the fighting in Europe, May 8, 1945.

Victory over Japan Sept. 2, 1945.

The United Nations officially organized 1945.

Cold war with Russia.

Attlee met Truman and Stalin at Potsdam.

Marshall Plan for rehabilitation strengthened Western Europe.

View of the South Portico showing the beautiful grounds and President Truman's balcony.

Philippines given independence.

Truman elected, 1948.

North Atlantic Treaty Organization, April 4, 1949.

North Korea invaded South Korea; United Nations assumed military defense, June 1950.

Truman did not try for reelection in 1952.

capital. Routines grew correspondingly. Truman, a dabbler in architecture, drew up plans for enlarging the Executive Offices and adding a small auditorium and a lunch bar for White House employees. The Senate opposed his plan and refused necessary appropriations. Truman then decided to build a balcony for family use, within the South Portico at the second floor level, leading off from the President's Oval Study. Many people were incensed. What right had any man to destroy the fine lines of the Portico's ancient design? Congress finally agreed to abide by the decision of William A. Delano, formerly of the Commission and the architect who "had done more work on the White House than any living man." Mr. Delano approved, saying that by making it possible to remove the ugly awnings "it would restore integrity to the six columns." At the same time a small moving picture theater was built under the East Terrace, and a small gymnasium next to the pool under the West Terrace.

80

Courtesy B. Altman & Co.

Decorator's sketch for President Truman's bed room.

For three and a half years of Truman's last Administration the family lived in Blair House while the White House was being restored. They were glad to return to the rebuilt White House for his last year. They went back to the most consistently furnished and by far the most comfortable and convenient living quarters the White House had ever known. Mrs. Truman said, "They have lighted up this whole floor, which was so dark before."

And for the first time in history the President of the United States had a built-in clothes closet!—spacious and well equipped.

All the second floor bedrooms were given much needed closets. The old wardrobes were removed. Cheerful printed cottons of the 18th Century types were used. When possible, furniture was refinished, reupholstered and used again. If new furniture was needed, reproductions of 18th Century models were used.

The "Williamsburg Floral Bough" is one of the attractive fabrics used on the second floor. →

The President's bedroom was done in spruce green, brown and beige, the colors of the old Regency chintz used for draperies. The bathroom, large, well-equipped. Walls green with white glass tiles.

In 1953 the President's bedroom was not changed.

81

Decorator's sketch for Mrs. Truman's sitting room.

Mrs. Truman's interest in bridge is shown in the bridge table and four chairs which is set up in constant readiness.

In 1953, Mrs. Eisenhower had this sitting room done over as her bedroom. And the former bedroom became her dressing room. Needed cupboards, mirrors and a dressing table were added.

It was surprising to find a shortage of storage space here. But the new First Lady had had to hang her Inauguration wardrobe in the Family Sitting Room on racks hastily brought from the cloak rooms!

For Mrs. Truman's sitting room, between her bedroom and that of the President, she chose a floral print of amethyst colored flowers and green leaves on an ivory ground. This was used for draperies and on several chairs. The walls were painted off-white with a hint of mauve. The floor covering was a deep plum. A harmonizing color in velvet covered important chairs.

Mrs. Truman's bedroom was done in gray, rose and blue, with mahogany furniture. Her bath had black and white squares on the wall and a black tub etched with a fan design.

Bess Truman would always have preferred the friendly social life of their home town to that of the White House. She made the necessary appearances and carried out her official duties but avoided the limelight. Her husband and her daughter were her first interests. She was said to be largely responsible for the President's decision not to seek another term.

Decorator's sketch for Margaret Truman's sitting room, 1952.

Opposite the Presidential suite was Margaret Truman's apartment. Her sitting room had dark green walls and greenish-white woodwork with a dark green rug. The charming Louis XVI print used at the windows and on some of the chairs suggested the pinks and greens and ivory white used to cover the other pieces. Her bedroom, hung with a pretty floral print, was in soft pink and ivory as was her tiny bathroom. Her piano was a gift from her father on her 10th birthday.

In 1953, by cleverly switching the decorations in these two identical rooms (see Second Floor Plan, page 89) Mrs. Eisenhower's bedroom was given the pale pinks and soft greens she so much likes.

Both rooms were repainted to the palest pink.

←— *The glazed chintz in green and rose on a cream ground is taken from a Louis XVI print called "The Triumph of Hymen."*

Courtesy B. Altman & Co.

Decorator's sketch for the West Hall Sitting Room, 1952.

The Family Sitting Room was given greater privacy with new partitions that separated it from the Center Corridor. New 18th Century style furniture added to the old was arranged comfortably before the great fan window.

← The red and cream toile, used at the window and on some furniture, is of the copper plate type so admired by Jefferson. First made in England in 1799, for the American trade, it is called "The Victory of Washington and the Apotheosis of Benjamin Franklin". Washington is in a leopard-drawn chariot with the Goddess of Independence. Franklin and the Goddess of Liberty carry the banner— "Where Liberty dwells there is my country".

In 1953 the Eisenhowers brought to this room their books, photographs and other special treasures. When there are no guests, the President and Mrs. Eisenhower have tray-suppers here and watch television. Theirs is the first color T V set in the White House.

Sometimes friends come in for bridge or canasta. Or they sing, with Mamie at the piano or the new electric organ her mother gave her.

Courtesy Scalamandré Silks, Inc.

84

Courtesy B. Altman & Co.

Decorator's sketch for the East Hall Sitting Room, 1952.

At the east end of the second floor corridor, between the Lincoln and Rose Rooms, is a room nearly identical with the family sitting room. It is used as a sitting room for the guest suite. Furnished in 18th Century reproductions it takes its color scheme from the emerald green satin damask with a lily-of-the-valley motif in biscuit, used for the draperies. Furniture was upholstered in figured biscuit silk velvet.

The emerald green satin damask with lily-of-the-valley in biscuit was specially woven. →

Courtesy F. Schumacher & Co.

The Second Floor Corridor, 1952.

The red and cream color scheme of the East Sitting Room was continued into the Center Corridor on chairs and sofas with cotton damask, stripes and toile. The new built-in breakfront bookcases and recessed ones with shell tops, the arrangement of comfortable chairs and tables, and the new chandelier make the big hall attractive and livable.

The Center Corridor is used as a less private living area by the family and house guests—for intimate parties and family gatherings, a place to talk with someone or to wait to go down to dinner.

*Top Floor Corridor, →
made pleasant with chintz covered chairs and sofas and book-filled built-in bookcases. Through the first right arched door is the Sun Room over the South Portico. Through the left arched doorway are ample storage rooms.*

On the third floor, four new guest bedrooms and baths were added to the eleven already there. These were never before fully furnished. The rooms are small and were kept simple but the attractive chintzes and furnishings were chosen with care. Some of them are reproductions from the famous Williamsburg Collection.

← *One of the simple but pleasant guest rooms, with 18th Century reproduction furniture and flowered curtains.*

Dwight D. Eisenhower 1953-

First Republican President in 20 years.

Favored lower tariffs.

Mamie's bangs started a vogue in hairstyle.

First hydrogen bomb test.

Korean Truce, July 27, 1953.

"Big Three" meeting in Bermuda.

Reception, Nov. 10, 1953, marked "official completion of the renovation." First use of newly finished East Entrance Hall.

Eisenhower proposed pooling nuclear resources, through a U.N. agency, for domestic uses and the common good.

Dwight D. Eisenhower and his wife, Mamie, came to the White House on the heels of the 1952 restoration. They found little reason to make changes. As an army wife, Mamie knew how to make the Eisenhowers at home in any quarters they were assigned.

Getting along with all kinds of people and in all situations was not new to Mamie. She had married a young, unknown lieutenant who became a five star general before he was President. Her easy manner, ready smile and a capacity for enjoyment, coupled with her innate dignity and kindliness would grace any First Lady.

Eisenhower, as President, found both advantages and disadvantages in his broad military experience. Through his achievements in World War II and as Supreme Commander of Allied Forces for N A T O he became internationally known and admired. He acquired an understanding of other nations. His military knowledge helped gain a truce in Korea. It enabled him to recognize that the growing effectiveness of nuclear weapons made radical changes in the make-up and uses of our military forces imperative.

But Eisenhower, new to government politics, had to learn the differences in military and political leadership. He was hampered by the party change-over and conflicts within his own party.

The Eisenhower Administration, though serious, industrious and orderly, began less as a crusade and with a slower pace than his followers had hoped. But toward the end of his first year, by calling on all nations in the U.N. to share in the development of atomic power for peaceful uses, Eisenhower gave promise of real leadership.

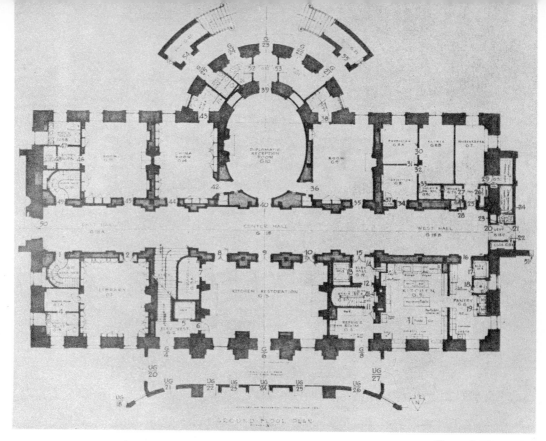

Ground Floor Plan

First Floor Plan

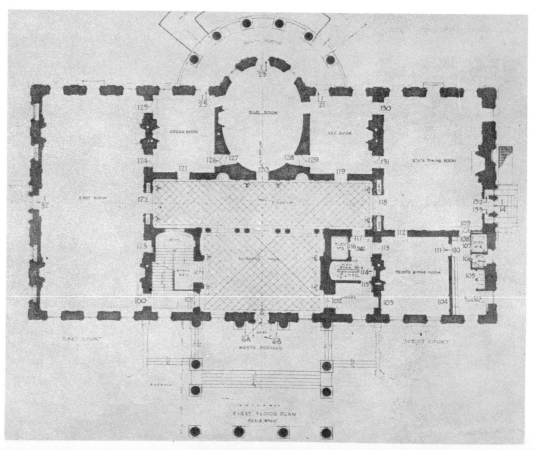

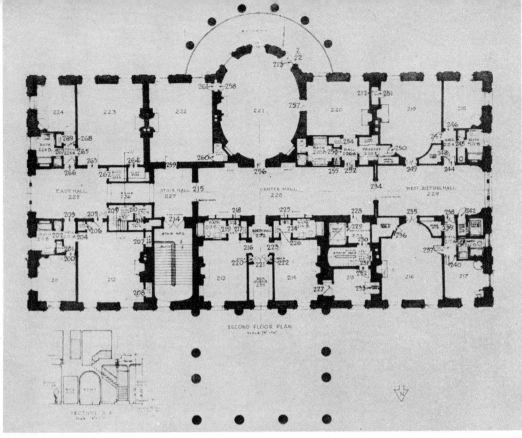

Second Floor Plan

Third Floor Plan

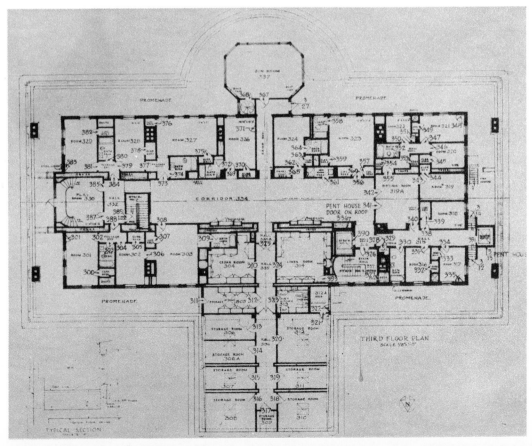

The Tour

Visitors who wish to see the public rooms of the White House enter the ground floor by way of the East Executive Avenue entrance. One passes along the East Wing corridor through a small room where there are portraits of Presidents Lincoln, Fillmore and Grant, into the ground floor corridor with its historic vaulted ceiling and new Vermont marble walls.

The Library

To the right of the entrance to the corridor is the Library. Here are housed the books given by the American Booksellers Association. Put down in this room to preserve it is a red rug made in the Coolidge Administration for the Red Room. It has the seal of the United States as its central motif.

The China Room

Beyond and across the hall is the China Room where Presidential china from the time of John Adams is displayed in built-in cupboards. This collection originated with Mrs. Harrison.

Wide World Photos, Inc.

In the fall of 1953 the East Entrance Hall was completed; new birch paneled walls and marble floors.

The Library. →
Around the fireplace opening are tiles showing scenes in the "Life of a President of the United States." They were designed by Franklin Roosevelt for his library at Hyde Park. When he died Mrs. Roosevelt left them by request for the White House.
The busts in the windows are of Lincoln and Harrison.

The Corridor.
← *Paneled into one wall, is a slab of marble with John Adams's famous prayer for the White House. The prayer was originally sent in a letter to his wife, Abigail, in 1800. Franklin Roosevelt had it carved across the great fireplace in the State Dining Room and in the restoration it was placed in the Corridor. (See page 96.)*

The China Room. →
The circular settee in the center of the room is upholstered to harmonize with the red dress in the painting of Mrs. Coolidge which hangs on the wall. The settee is from the gilt furniture Buchanan bought for the Blue Room in 1857. The pair of standard candelabra were used in the White House by Monroe. In the window is a bust of Truman. The vases by the fireplace are from Arthur's time.

During the renovation the Library and four other ground floor rooms were paneled in boards cut from the original White House timbers. (These had been replaced with steel.) Fireplace mantels were carved of this wood also. The boards were finished to a lovely color and the old nail holes left to add interest and pattern.

1952   Reconstruction cost about $6,750,000.

J. Adams

Washington

Madison

Monroe

Garfield

Pierce

J. Q. Adams

Wilson

T. Roosevelt

F. Roosevelt

Truman

Lincoln

Truman

Presidential China.

Wilson, Franklin Roosevelt and Trum
photos, courtesy Lenox, I

The Diplomatic Reception Room.

Wide World Photos, Inc.

The Diplomatic Reception Room

The ground floor Oval Room directly under the oval Blue Room is the Diplomatic Reception Room. Over its door is the Presidential Seal, which Theodore Roosevelt had inlaid in the floor of the Front Entrance Hall, moved because recent Presidents were troubled at its being walked on. The seal is bronze inlaid in marble. This room is used on social occasions by officials and distinguished guests as a men's dressing room. Portraits of White House hostesses hang on its walls. It was from this room that Franklin Roosevelt broadcast most of his "Fireside Chats."

The ground floor rooms were decorated thriftily; old furniture was refinished and recovered and some of the old drapery fabrics from the State rooms were recut and used for the windows.

The new marble stairway opposite the China Room leads to the first floor.

The East Room

Here to the right of the small stair hall is the East Reception Room, the largest and most magnificent of the rooms in the White House. The nation's most formal and brilliant social life centers here. In this beautiful gold and white setting foreign celebrities are honored, State and Diplomatic Receptions are held, balls, musicales and gala entertainments. Presidents' daughters have been married here. In Lincoln's time war worn soldiers slept here. Large and important conferences have been held here. The East Room has been decked with flowers, arrayed in bunting, hung with huge maps and the flags of allied nations. And it has been shrouded with black for the Presidents whose bodies lay here in state. *(See pages 26-31)*

Time for building 2½ years; began in 1949, completed in 1952.

The Commission, who was responsible for all decisions, was made up of two members of the Senate, two members of the House, and two appointed by the President.

Executive Director, Major General Glen E. Edgerton.

Consulting architect, William A. Delano.

New structural frame of concrete and 660 tons of steel built into the original shell.

10,000 cubic yards of earth excavated.

$868,000 bomb shelter erected.

Formerly 48 full rooms and 14 baths.

Now 54 full rooms and 16 baths (almost as many lavatories).

The utility sub-basement includes an incinerator, air conditioner, small laundry, small barber shop, a small dentist's office, servants' dining room, and ample storage space.

All rooms given air-conditioning including the sun-room on the roof.

Electric master clock control.

Central vacuum cleaning system.

A motion picture room.

Five elevators, formerly one.

23 kinds of marble and stone were used in the White House from 16 quarries in 13 States.

Dates of White House embedded in the floor of the North Entrance Hall: Laying of the Cornerstone 1792; Restoration dates, 1817, 1902, 1952.

The Green Room

The Green Room connects the East Room with the Blue Room. This is one of the two smaller parlors used for informal receptions and for family gatherings and friendly talk. It was originally intended for the "Common Dining Room" and was probably so used through Madison's time. In Monroe's day it was called the Card Room, and the President and his friends often sat here late into the night, playing cards. *(See pages 47-49)*

The Blue Room

Famous for its oval shape the Blue Room has been thought by many people to be the most beautiful room in the White House. The Blue Room is the President's Reception Room. In this room at Receptions the President and the First Lady stand to shake hands with each of their guests as they pass in line. Here the President receives foreign diplomats coming to present their credentials and guests for smaller state dinners and receptions. White House weddings have been held here. Grover Cleveland was married in the Blue Room. *(See pages 18-23)*

The Red Room

The Red Room is identical in size and shape with the Green Room. It is used by the President's wife to receive guests. Because of its warm colors and more intimate size, it is a charming room for smaller gatherings, teas, family parties and conversation by the fire. Guests for smaller dinners are received here. Hayes took the oath of office here. Originally the Red Room was the President's Ante-Chamber since it adjoined the room to the west which was then the Library and Cabinet Room. *(See pages 44-46)*

The State Dining Room

This southwest corner room is now the State Dining Room. It is the second largest room in the White House and, since the 1902 restoration when it was enlarged, it can comfortably seat 100 people at luncheon or dinner. The great and near great of America and the world have sat down to dinners, from those as comparatively simple as the wartime fare to sumptuous 13-course dinners with fine vintage wines and the most elaborate floral decorations complementing the gorgeous gold centerpiece. *(See pages 63-65)*

The North Entrance Hall

A 70-foot corridor, upon which the State Rooms face, extends between the State Dining Room and the East Room. Over the Blue Room door President Truman placed a full color plaster model of the President's Seal. He designed it with 48 stars and faced the eagle away from the arrows, the symbol of war, toward the olive branches, the symbol of peace.

East of the Entrance Hall is the gracious, newly designed Main Stairway. Visitors go out through the Front Entrance under the North Portico with its beautiful new planting of boxwood.

Looking back at the stately dignity of the White House, which has witnessed more than a century and a half of living, storms, fires, wars and progress; recalling the stirring events and far-reaching decisions it has known; the men and women whose lives, while dedicated to their country, knew the griefs and joys common to every man—it is easy to agree with Theodore Roosevelt that, "It is a good thing to preserve such buildings as historic monuments which keep alive our sense of continuity with the nation's past."

"I pray Heaven to bestow the best of the blessings on this house and all that hereafter inhabit it. May none but honest and wise men ever rule under this roof."

Prayer written by President John Adams.